BEYOND BIRDING

Field Projects for Inquisitive Birders

Thomas C. Grubb, Jr.

Department of Zoology
The Ohio State University
Columbus, Ohio 43210

THE BOXWOOD PRESS

Illustrations by Vicki Vaughn

© 1986
by
The Boxwood Press

Distributed
by

The Boxwood Press
183 Ocean View Blvd.
Pacific Grove, CA 93950

408—375-9110

ISBN: 0-940168-02-2

Grubb, Thomas C.
   Beyond Birding.

   Bibliography: p.
   1. Ornithology—Field work. I. Title.
QL677.5.G78   1986   598′.072   86-25889
ISBN 0-940168-02-2

Printed in U.S.A.

To Jill

Contents

Preface

ONE of the more influential field studies of birds ever performed was conducted just north of my university here in Columbus. While carrying on her duties as wife, mother and homemaker, Mrs. Margaret Morse Nice devoted many hours to studying the behavior and ecology of Song Sparrows. Mrs. Nice's account of her work is generally regarded as one of the finer examples of descriptive ornithology ever published in North America by anyone, amateur or professional.

At the time of Mrs. Nice's study, amateurs were routinely making important contributions to ornithology. General conclusions they reached from their field work were useful additions to the body of knowledge about birds. However, from the 1950s on, as the study of avian biology became more analytical and less descriptive, contributions by amateurs became less pivotal to the discipline. One of the functions of this book is to bring the techniques of analytical ornithology to the amateur student of birds.

Descriptive ornithology, which Mrs. Nice accomplished so beautifully, requires careful observation and note-taking on the behavior of birds in their natural environment. The next step is to look for generalities, common attributes about the events seen. For example, after a number of years of watching the Song Sparrows she had color-banded, Mrs. Nice could generalize that in Columbus, Ohio, only males of the species stayed on the breeding ground all winter.

Very often, the final step in descriptive ornithology is to create some explanation, or hypothesis, for why the generality discovered should exist. To continue with the Song Sparrow example, we might suggest that males wintering in the breeding area are more likely to secure a breeding territory during the following spring. The processes of natural selection, therefore, should favor male Song Sparrows wintering in Columbus because those birds would produce more offspring during their lifetimes than would male Song Sparrows that went south for the winter. Increased reproductive success the following spring, then, is a hypothesis for what causes some males to overwinter at the northern breeding site.

Although there are a few exceptions, it seems fair to say that most amateur ornithologists have not progressed beyond the descriptive stage of the science to the next stage, which is analytical ornithology. At the core of analytical ornithology is a method for evaluating hypotheses. In particular, analytical ornithology provides a method for concluding when a hypothesis is wrong, when an explanation of cause and effect is a mistake. In our Song Sparrow example, the methods of analytical ornithology would give us a way of concluding whether we should believe that males stay north because they have a better chance of subsequently securing a breeding territory the next spring. It is this ability to detect incorrect hypotheses that makes analytical ornithology such an advance over the descriptive study of birds.

This book presents the concepts and methods of analytical ornithology by analyzing a series of hypotheses: Northern Orioles prefer to build their nests over water; the size of a woodlot determines how many species of birds live there; White-breasted Nuthatches cache food during the fall in the same parts of a woodland where they will be foraging during the winter, and so forth. After the reader works through several of the chapters, he or she should be able to appreciate the steps involved in analyzing hypotheses and should grasp the general concepts of determining when a hypothesis is wrong.

With the idea of making the practice of analytical ornithology attractive and accessible, I have organized this book into four major sections. Chapter 1 takes a detailed look at how analytical procedures can be applied to the field study of birds. Chapter 2 examines in greater depth the concepts and principles of analytical science. The remaining chapters suggest how to go about analyzing hypotheses about where birds live, how they coexist, and why they make the decisions they do. Most chapters conclude with a few sources of further reading taken from North American ornithological journals. The last major section of the book, Appendices 1 and 2, contains methods for performing certain elementary statistical tests of hypotheses. As explained further in Chapter 2, knowledge of how likely an outcome is due to chance is very important in determining whether a hypothesis is wrong. Analytical statistics can help determine the probability that a finding is due to chance. As an option, a statistical test can be used in conjunction with the results obtained in every project. At the end of each chapter, the appropriate statistical analysis is outlined.

None of the projects outlined requires extensive travel, and many can be taken up whenever a few minutes or hours become available. The ability to recognize individual birds is not a prerequisite for any project. In any case, capturing and marking birds in any way is illegal without federal and state permits. Equipment needs have been kept to a minimum. Many projects require only a pencil, notebook, binoculars, and watch. In a few cases, some simple, homemade devices are needed.

This book is intended for several audiences. First, it is designed for amateur birders, some of whom may now be involved in descriptive ornithological endeavors, such as Christmas Counts and Breeding Bird Surveys. This group of "non-traditional students" includes some of the very keenest observers of free-ranging birds, and their observations can be invaluable in amassing the facts from which hypotheses can be formulated. Yet amateurs have rarely combined descriptive and analytical ornithology. This book will have served its purpose if it broadens the perspective of the amateur concerning the various ways that the science of ornithology can be pursued.

The second major audience is the high school biology and science student. Aside from being intrinsically interesting and "low-cost" subjects for class projects or independent study, the exercises to follow could serve as models for how any kind of analytical science is performed, and what its capabilities and limitations are.

The third major intended audience is the students taking college-level courses in ornithology, animal behavior, and/or ecology. The analytically oriented projects should be useful adjuncts to many lecture topics in these disciplines of biology. Many of these field projects can be pursued during the fall, winter, and early spring when colleges are in session.

Among the many teachers who have guided my own interests in field biology, I especially wish to acknowledge John T. Emlen and Jack P. Hailman of the University of Wisconsin-Madison, and Kenneth Rawson of Swarthmore College. All or part of various drafts of this book were reviewed by Constance Bart, Jonathon Bart, Bruce Peterjohn, and Daniel R. Petit. These friends and colleagues have my deep thanks. I appreciate the vigilance of John L. Crites, my department chairman, in keeping my teaching load sufficiently low that I had time to pursue these ideas. While preparing this book, I was supported periodically by several grants from the U.S. National Science Foundation and the U.S. Department of Agriculture. Finally, I thank Margaret Jill Grubb for our discussions about this book's ideas, and for many other things.

Thomas C. Grubb, Jr.

September, 1986
Columbus, Ohio

1

Ornithology as a Science

S UPPOSE we have come to a great marsh or swamp to spend a
day watching water birds. After scanning the habitat and,
perhaps, taking notes on the kinds and numbers of the birds
present, we sit in the sun on an old log eating our sandwiches, and
get to wondering why so many wading birds have white feathers.
Great Egrets, Snowy Egrets and immature Little Blue Herons are
all covered in white plumage. Someone ventures that perhaps white
feathers help the birds catch fish because they reflect the blue of the
sky down into the water, making the white bird match its
background. Somebody else suggests that if white feathers have
evolved only because they fool fish, then all white birds should feed
on fish. We all begin to leaf through our field guides, calling out
white-feathered species and what they eat. White-tailed Tropicbird,
White Pelican, and Gannet all eat fish. Then we come to the swans,
which are white, but eat vegetation. We try another idea, that white
feathers are only possessed by birds that eat any aquatic food. This
would take care of the swan problem.
Off we go again through our
field guides, but not far.
Snow Geese are
white, yet they
graze on land. As
our lunch ends,
we conclude that
we do not have any firm
idea why birds are white, but we are

1

sure it is not solely because they eat aquatic food. Whooping
Cranes and Ivory Gulls are also white and eat aquatic food, but
Snow Geese disobey the rule, so the rule, as it stands, must be
wrong.

Over our lunch, we have just engaged in *analytical ornithology*.
We have used the scientific method to investigate a property of
nature. The scientific method is a system which creates a general
statement about some natural phenomenon, then assesses it
systematically. The general statement is called a *hypothesis*. It is
created by combining previously unrelated bits of knowledge in a
new way. We then evaluate the hypothesis by making a prediction
that we can test. The test will tell us if the prediction is true or false.
If the prediction is false, the hypothesis must also be false. If the
prediction turns out to be true, we do not know whether the
hypothesis is true or false; only that we could not disprove it.

Analytical ornithology uses the scientific method to test hypotheses about the lives of birds. In order to gain a better appreciation
of how this method works, let's translate our lunch-time thinking
into components of the scientific method. We saw white birds in the
swamp, and we knew from our reading or from first-hand
observation that they ate fish. From these two pieces of information, one of us answered our question about white feathers by
creating the hypothesis that all white birds eat fish. We then
predicted that if all white birds eat fish, all the white birds in our
field guides must eat fish. We tested the prediction by paging
through while noting what each white-feathered species ate. The
swans proved the prediction false, so the hypothesis had to be false.
This outcome was not unusual; a large proportion of hypotheses in
science are proven false. We had only to create a new hypothesis
accounting for the swans. We stated that all white birds eat aquatic
food, animal and/or vegetable. We disproved this second hypothesis, too, with the Snow Geese, but let's for a moment pretend we
didn't. Let's pretend we failed to find the Snow Goose, ptarmigan,
and Snowy Owl. We would have gone through the entire field

guide noting that every other white bird we found ate aquatic prey. We would then have proven true the prediction that every white bird in our field guides ate aquatic food. Would we have proven true the hypothesis that all white birds on earth eat aquatic food? No; we would only have failed to prove it false. Somewhere in the highlands of Sumatra or in the vast expanse of Siberia, there could be a white-feathered species that does not eat aquatic food. Until we noticed Snow Geese, ptarmigan, and Snowy Owls, we could only say that we had not been able to show the hypothesis was false, but that we never could prove that it was absolutely true. This conclusion indicates a very important attribute held in common by all branches of science. In a real sense, nothing in all of science is true; there are only some things we have failed to disprove. Figure 1.1 illustrates how the scientific method is used to test hypotheses,

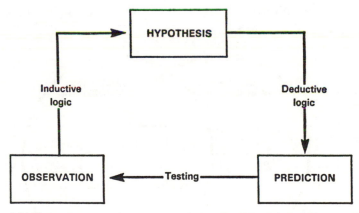

Fig. 1.1. Components and processes of the scientific method. Observations, including the results of previous testing, are combined inductively into a hypothesis of cause and effect. From this hypothesis, one or more particular predictions are deduced. The validity of each prediction is evaluated by empirical testing. If the testing proves the prediction false, then the parent hypothesis must also be false. If the test proves the prediction true, then the test has also failed to disprove the parent hypothesis, and our belief is strengthened that the parent hypothesis *might* be true. In science, a hypothesis cannot be proven to be true, it can only be proven to be not true. As the results of testing are observations, they can then be used in formulating new hypotheses, thus continuing the circuitous nature of the scientific method.

and Figure 1.2 depicts the relationships of descriptive and analytical ornithology to the components of the scientific method.

Incidentally, on snowy winter evenings, it can be quite enjoyable to play the game of making hypotheses and testing them with field guides. For example, females are always less colorful than males. Within a taxonomic family, forest birds are always brighter than open-country birds. Juveniles always resemble females in color, never males. Birds of coniferous woods are always brighter than those of deciduous forest. The higher the latitude, the more seabird species and the fewer land bird species are found. More species reach a limit to their range in Kansas than anywhere else in North America.

Used properly, the scientific method is a very powerful tool for the ornithologist because it tells him or her when a mistake has been made. In the succeeding chapters on field ornithology, I will advance a number of hypotheses and suggest methods for determining whether they are wrong.

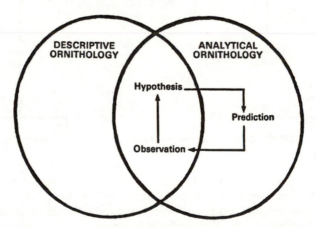

Fig. 1.2. Components of the scientific method contained within descriptive ornithology and analytical ornithology. For simplicity, the processes of inductive logic, deductive logic, and testing have been omitted here, but see Fig. 1.1. Hypothesis and Observation are within the domains of both types of ornithology. However, Prediction and the associated deductive logic and testing are found only within the realm of analytical ornithology.

Further reading.

Ainley, M. G. 1980. The contribution of the amateur to North American ornithology: a historical perspective. *Living Bird* 18:161-177.

Mayfield, H. F. 1978. The amateur in ornithology. *Auk* 96:168-171.

McCrimmon, D. A., Jr. and A. Sprunt IV. (eds.). 1978. Proceedings of a conference on the amateur and North American ornithology. Ithaca, New York Cornell Laboratory of Ornithology.

2

Analytical Ornithology

IN the Preface, I mentioned the descriptive study of Song Sparrows made by Mrs. Margaret Morse Nice, and noted that I planned to illustrate procedures that would show how descriptive ornithology, such as Mrs. Nice's research, could lead to the analytical phase of hypothesis-testing.

In order to do ornithology of an analytical, hypothesis-testing nature, we need to employ analytical statistics. The word statistic means a numerical fact, a measurement. Any statistic is classified as being either descriptive or analytical. Descriptive statistics measure by describing something and analytical statistics measure by comparing things. Why do we need statistics at all? In the Chapter 1 example of white birds and aquatic food, we tested predictions without using any statistics. In general, the reason we need statistics is so we can deal with the variation shown by all biological phenomena. Let's explore further the idea of variation in biology. Suppose I asked you to tell me how tall American Woodcocks are, or how red male Northern Cardinals are, or how loudly American Robins sing. First, you would have to decide what unit of measurement to use, centimeters of height for the woodcocks, wavelength of light for the cardinals, decibels of sound for the robins. However, you would encounter a problem immediately. You would find that no two woodcocks were exactly the same height, no two cardinals exactly the same color, and no two robins exactly the same loudness. Indeed, for our test of white birds and aquatic food, we assumed that all species of white birds were the same "whiteness," an assumption which is unlikely to be true.

In ornithology, we have the problem of how to describe things which are variable. We respond to this problem by using, together, two kinds of descriptive statistics, *measures of central tendency* and *measures of dispersion*. One measure of central tendency everyone knows is the *average*. Familiar examples are baseball players' batting averages, average annual family income, and average monthly rainfall. The average, known in science as the *mean*, is a statistic which describes the central tendency of a group of values. The mean equals the sum of the values in a group divided by the number of values in that group. Other descriptive measures of central tendency are the *median*, which is the middle value in a group, and the *mode*, which is the most frequent value in a group.

Measures of dispersion are the second major form of descriptive statistic. The best known measure of dispersion is called the *variance*. It reveals how much variation exists among the values clustered about a mean or average, that is, how spread out those values are. Two groups of values with the same mean can have quite different variances, as illustrated in Fig. 2.1. As a further

Fig. 2.1. **Imaginary means and variances.** Parts **A** and **B** of the figure show imagined groups of values. The size of a value increases from left to right along the horizontal axes, and the number of values increases from bottom to top along the vertical axes. The two groups of values have identical means, but the values in group **B** are more dispersed about the mean. Because of this greater variation, group **B** would have a larger calculated variance than would group **A**.

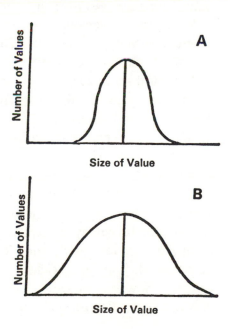

example, consider two unusual decks of playing cards. One deck contains only fours, fives and sixes, while the second deck has aces (ones) through nines. Now suppose that you drew one card from a deck, wrote down its value, replaced it in the deck, shuffled the cards thoroughly, then drew another card in the same way, and you did this over and over for each of the two decks. You would find that your samples of values from both decks had just about the same mean of five, but that their measures of dispersion were different. The sample from the deck with aces through nines would have the greater variation in values, the greater variance. The variance is simply a mathematical way of describing how extensively values are spread about the mean or average.

The amateur ornithologists of Mrs. Nice's era and earlier were quite comfortable using descriptive statistics like the mean, as we all are. The disadvantage from which amateurs have had difficulty recovering arose when ornithology became an analytical, hypothesis-testing science as well as continuing to be a descriptive one. At that point, more involved procedures termed *analytical statistics* were called upon to overcome the problems posed by the variation inherent in biological records. This chapter and this book will consider these analytical statistics.

Analytical statistics are necessary tools for testing predictions. Indeed, it seems we find predictions fascinating not only in ornithology or biology, but in almost any field of endeavor. Here are a few representative hypotheses and their predictions. If your nephew had earned his Master's degree (hypothesis), he would now be earning a higher salary (prediction). If the combined French and Spanish fleet had not been positioned perpendicular to Nelson's ships-of-the-line (hypothesis), it would have triumphed at Trafalgar (prediction). If I cut my fingernails (hypothesis), I won't wear holes in my gloves so fast (prediction). Two of these predictions cannot be tested; they are not scientific predictions. In the fingernails example, however, we can compare what would happen to my gloves if I cut my fingernails with what would happen if I did not cut my fingernails. That is, we can establish a controlled test of the prediction to determine whether it is true or false. This procedure of evaluating a prediction (and, thereby, a hypothesis) by means of a controlled test is the heart of doing analytical science of any kind. If you perform a controlled test of a hypothesis, you are doing analytical science. If you don't, you're not. We will never be able to test the predictions about the Spanish-French fleet or about your nephew's Master's degree because a controlled test is impossible. The distinction between doing analytical science and doing any other intellectual pursuit is hard, clear, and permanent.

Analytical ornithologists evaluate hypotheses by subjecting the hypotheses' predictions to testing. Why are analytical statistics necessary for these tests? They are necessary because they help us to decide whether any test result is real, or could be due just to an error in sampling. Suppose we consider the hypothesis, based on physiological principles, that within a bird species, body size is inversely related to environmental temperature. That is, the colder the environment, the larger the individuals of a given species that live in that environment will be. Such a hypothesis is known to ecologists as Bergmann's Rule. What testable predictions can we deduce from this hypothesis? One prediction might be that, since average annual temperature drops progressively from the equator to the poles, any North American bird species with a large latitudinal range, the Northern Bobwhite for instance, should be represented by smaller individuals in the southern part of its range than in the northern part. Let's say we test this prediction by capturing and weighing samples of bobwhites in Alabama and Ohio. We will prove true the prediction and support the hypothesis (Bergmann's Rule) if the Ohio birds are heavier than the Alabama birds. Here is where a problem immediately arises which can only be solved with analytical statistics. The problem occurs because there isn't just one size bobwhite in Ohio and one size in Alabama. If there were only one size in each place, it would be easy to tell whether Ohio birds were larger, but in both places there will be

variation in the size of bobwhites in our samples, and
this variation is the problem
because it can have either
of two causes. The
variation can be real,
it can truly reflect
the variation in size of all
the bobwhites in Ohio or
Alabama, or it can be the
result of sampling error,
a sample of bobwhite weights that does not reflect the variation of
weights within a whole state-wide population. From our sample of
weights taken in each state, we can calculate a measure of central
tendency such as the mean, and a measure of dispersion such as the
variance. If the two means are different, the question we have to
deal with is this: Are they different because bobwhites in Ohio and
Alabama really are of different size, or are they different because,
purely by chance, we happened to draw heavy birds from one state
and lighter birds from the other state. Fig. 2.2 illustrates the
uncertainty that increasing variance introduces into the testing of
predictions. For simplicity, Fig. 2.2 ignores the known difference in
weights between male and female bobwhites.

This point about the sources of variation is important enough to
be approached another way. Suppose you have two jars, each
containing 1,000 red or white marbles. How would you test the
hypothesis that one jar has a higher percentage of red marbles than
the other? The surest way, of course, would be to count every last
red marble in each jar. Then you could be absolutely sure whether
the hypothesis was correct, but suppose you don't have enough
time to make a complete count and you must evaluate the
hypothesis based on samples of only 100 marbles from each jar.
You could then predict that if one jar has a higher percentage of red
marbles, then a sample of 100 marbles from that jar should have

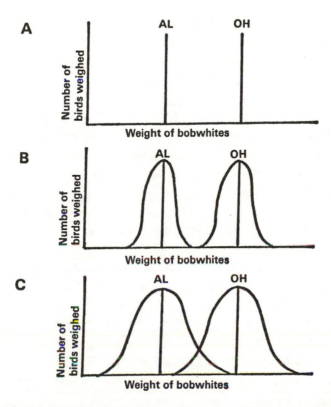

Fig. 2.2. Imaginary means and variances of the weights of Northern Bobwhites in Alabama and Ohio. In parts A, B, and C, the vertical lines indicate the positions of the mean weights in Alabama and Ohio. The mean values for birds from each state are identical in all three parts of the figure. In part A, all birds in the same state have the same weight. Because the variance in part A is zero, it appears safe to conclude that Ohio birds are heavier. In part B, some intra-state variation in weights is evident, but because every Ohio bobwhite sampled was heavier than every Alabama bobwhite sampled, it still seems reasonable to conclude that there is a real difference between Alabama and Ohio in the weight of Northern Bobwhites. In part C, the variation within a state is extensive, and some Alabama birds sampled were heavier than some Ohio birds sampled. Because the resulting variances are large, we cannot be sure, initially, whether a real difference exists between the weights of Alabama and Ohio bobwhites in spite of the overlap between the two samples of weights. The use of analytical statistics provides a method for determining whether we should believe that the difference between the means shown in part C is real, or whether we should conclude that the difference could have been caused solely by chance sampling error.

more red ones than a sample of 100 marbles from the second jar. Let's imagine we take the two samples and find that in one case, 25 of the 100 marbles are red, while in the second case, 35 of the 100 are red. We are aware that in each sample the percentage of red marbles is probably not exactly the same as the percentage of red marbles in the whole jar. The 10% difference in the proportion of red marbles in the samples from the two jars could have occurred either because one jar actually contained a higher percentage of red marbles, or it could have been caused solely by chance. To belabor the obvious, the two jars could represent Ohio and Alabama and the marbles could denote bobwhites, with the simplification that each state has only "big" or "little" bobwhites, not the continuous range of sizes we see in the real world.

Are we dealing with a difference in weights of bobwhites between Alabama and Ohio, or with a chance event? We must know the likelihood of a chance outcome being responsible before we can declare the prediction true or false. The use of analytical statistics tells us this likelihood, the probability that the difference we found was due to random chance events associated with taking a small sample from a large population. Suppose we find that the Ohio bobwhites we sample have a higher mean weight than that of the birds in our sample from Alabama, as illustrated in Fig. 2.2. Analytical statistics can tell us what the probability is that the difference in weights was due to sampling error. If that probability is very low, we might confidently support the prediction that the average bobwhite in Ohio is larger than the average Alabama bird.

Ornithologists and many other scientists have adopted what is called the 5% *level of confidence*. This means that if the probability is 5% or less that a difference between two samples could be due to chance alone, then the difference is considered to be real, actually to exist in nature. If the probability is greater than 5% that chance alone could have caused the difference, the difference is not considered to be real. Because of this procedure, ornithologists and other scientists have an objective basis for rejecting or failing to reject hypotheses. That is, they have a method for determining which explanations about nature they should believe. An optional section at the end of each of the following 20 projects in field ornithology involves using analytical statistics and the 5% level of confidence to evaluate hypotheses about the behavior and ecology of wild birds.

Further reading

Nice, M. M. 1964. Studies in the life history of the Song Sparrow. 2 volumes Dover, New York. (These are unabridged republications in paperback of the two volumes first published by the Linnaean Society of New York in 1937 and 1943.)

3

Do Woodpeckers Have
Preferred Heights for Digging Holes?

WOODPECKERS are primary cavity users, meaning they will only roost or nest in a cavity they have dug themselves in a dead limb, snag, or stump. In many woodlands almost every dead tree contains a woodpecker hole, and it has been claimed that the quantity of usable snags limits the number of woodpeckers in any forested area. We know that the different woodpecker species tend to dig their holes at different heights. Perhaps, the species living together have evolved different preferred heights to reduce competition. Unfortunately, we do not know if something else besides height is responsible for each species preference. For instance, it could be that Downy Woodpeckers always choose a location where the wood has partially rotted to the preferred degree. If we had some way of making the composition of a snag constant, then we could be more certain that the distance from the ground at which Downy Woodpeckers dig their cavities is a function of height only. It has recently been found that this species prefers artificial trees made of polystyrene beadboard to real trees for digging roost holes. Polystyrene beadboard is a material of homogeneous composition. It has no soft or hard spots. Blanks made from this material can be used to test the hypothesis that Downy Woodpeckers have a preferred height for excavating roost holes.

Three polystyrene blocks 15 cm by 15 cm square are required. (cm is the abbreviation for centimeter; 1 cm = 0.4 inches.) Downy Woodpeckers are known to dig holes in such square "trees." One block should be 120 cm long, one 240 cm, and one 360 cm. If you cannot find polystyrene blocks of this shape, you can make them by cutting 2.5-cm or 5-cm thick housing insulation into slabs of the proper size and gluing them together into blocks with panelling or linoleum glue. Paint them dark brown with latex, not leaded, paint.

Our hypothesis is really two hypotheses. The first hypothesis states that Downy Woodpeckers have a preferred tree height for their holes. The second hypothesis holds that on a tree of any particular height, the woodpeckers prefer to dig a certain distance from the snag top. Both of these hypotheses can be tested with the three polystyrene blanks.

Select a backyard or woods that you know contains Downy Woodpeckers. Within this area, pound three stout wooden poles or metal fence posts into the ground 3 m (meters) apart in a triangle formation. Then tie one polystyrene blank vertically to each pole with wire or rope. As often as you have time, ideally once a day, drop by to check for holes in the blanks and record your findings in Table 3.1. You may find that a bird starts several holes before it settles on one to excavate fully. Wait until one hole has been dug down to at least 10 cm below the bottom lip of the entrance before deciding that the Downy has made a clear-cut choice. Then record in Table 3.2 the distance from the top of the blank to the lower lip of the entrance.

How much confidence can we place in the choice of one bird? We cannot have too much confidence, because that bird may not be typical of the population as a whole. Therefore, repeat the procedure in several backyards or woodlots. Every bird excavating in the same place will increase our confidence in the hypotheses. However, we now have an uncontrolled variable; one or more of the "trees" have peck marks and cavities in them, and these must be filled in before each repetition of the experiment. To fill them in, file or plane off particles from a spare piece of polystyrene bead-board. A Stanley "surform" plane is excellent for this job. Soak the polystyrene particles in a slurry of equal parts Elmer's "carpenters' glue" and water. Dip out spoonsful of soaked particles and pack the holes and peck marks flush with the surface. After the fillings are dry and have been repainted, you are ready to test another bird. As you accumulate records, add them to Tables 3.1 and 3.2.

If all or almost all birds dig cavities in one of the three tree heights, their behavior will support the hypothesis that Downy Woodpeckers have a snag height preference. It is very possible that results will be less clear-cut, with some cavities dug in each "tree" type. Does this mean there is no preference? By following the statistical analysis described at the end of this chapter, you can decide whether your results are solely due to a chance outcome.

With this system of artificial trees, a number of other hypotheses becomes accessible to testing. For example, Downy Woodpeckers respond to cold winter weather by digging deeper cavities than they do in the summer. Male and female Downy Woodpeckers prefer different heights for excavating. Downy Woodpeckers orient their entrance holes away from the prevailing wind direction in winter. Since number of snags limits populations of primary cavity users, adding artificial trees to a woodland will increase the density (birds per hectare, say) of woodpeckers. The hectare (ha) is the metric unit commonly used in science to measure large areas. One hectare equals 10,000 m², or 2.47 acres. Can you think of other hypotheses?

Statistical analysis.

Appendix 1 details the purpose and procedures of statistical tests of hypotheses. Some imaginary results of Downy Woodpeckers' choices of tree height are used to explain the Chi-square Test of Goodness of Fit. Fill in Table 3.3 with your results and then follow the directions in Appendix 1 for deciding whether to reject the hypothesis that Downy Woodpeckers have a preferred tree height for excavating cavities. Degrees of freedom will equal two.

Further reading.

Grubb, T. C., Jr. 1982. Downy Woodpecker sexes select different cavity sites: an experiment using artificial snags. *Wilson Bulletin* **94**:577-579.

Kilham, L. 1977. Nest-site differences between Red-headed and Red-bellied Woodpeckers in South Carolina. *Wilson Bulletin* **89**:164-165.

Peterson, A. W. and T. C. Grubb, Jr. 1983. Artificial trees as a cavity substrate for woodpeckers. *Journal of Wildlife Management* **47**:790-798.

Short, L. L. 1979. Burdens of the picid hole-excavating habit. *Wilson Bulletin* **91**:16-28.

Table 3.1. Heights of artificial trees in which Downy Woodpeckers dug cavities

Cavity	Tree height (cm)		
	120	240	360
1			
2			
3			
4			
5			
6			
7			
8			
9			
10			
11			
12			
13			
14			
15			
16			
17			
18			
19			
20			

Table 3.2. Distance in centimeters between the top of an artificial tree and the lower lip of a cavity entrance

Cavity	Distance (cm)						
	0-25	26-50	51-75	76-100	101-125	126-150	151-175
1							
2							
3							
4							
5							
6							
7							
8							
9							
10							
11							
12							
13							
14							
15							
16							
17							
18							
19							
20							

Table 3.3. Observed and expected tree heights used by cavity-digging Downy Woodpeckers

	Number of birds choosing 120-cm trees	Number of birds choosing 240-cm trees	Number of birds choosing 360-cm trees
Observed in your study			
Expected due to chance alone			

4

How High a Song Perch?

During the breeding season, open-country birds use several techniques to broadcast song and defend territories. Horned Larks sing while circling high above their territories for minutes on end. Meadowlarks often sing and "rattle" during short flights near the ground, and deliver songs from perches. Savannah, Field and other sparrows rarely sing in flight, but spend considerable time on perches. Some workers have maintained that otherwise perfectly suitable habitat will not be colonized by certain grassland birds unless it contains a minimum complement of song perches such as scattered saplings, fence posts, or even mail boxes.

Currently, there is disagreement over preferred perch heights of open-country birds. One body of evidence suggests that all grassland birds prefer to sing and survey their territories from the highest available perch. Other work argues for a more complicated division of preferred perch heights among species living together. This project will test the hypothesis that different grassland species prefer different perch heights. Our general procedure will be similar to that of the preceding experiment with cavity site in Downy Woodpeckers, but this time we will deal with comparisons between species. You will need three boards, each about 3 cm square and 240 cm long (that is, three 8-foot "two-by-twos"), which can be purchased at any lumberyard, four 10-cm-long (4-inch) nails, a saw, hammer, hatchet, step ladder, and a pair of binoculars.

21

Perches of four heights can be fashioned from the 3-cm-square boards by cutting them as shown in Figure 4.1. Sharpen one end of the 60-, 120-, 180-, and 240-cm sticks with the hatchet and nail a 30-cm-long piece to the other end so it forms a "T."

Locate an open grassland in your area which contains several breeding species, such as Bobolink, Eastern Meadowlark, Red-winged Blackbird and/or Field Sparrow. Pastureland, hay fields, prairie, reclaimed strip-mined land, and salt marsh are possibilities. Carry your perches, ladder and hammer to a spot a good distance from the nearest existing perch site. Arrange the four perches so they form a square 3 m on a side, then pound them 33 cm into the ground so the tops of the Ts are 30, 90, 150, and 210 cm high.

Now you are ready to collect records. Retreat a considerable distance, find a comfortable post, rock, or lawn chair to lean

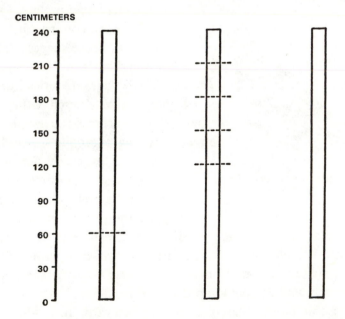

Fig. 4.1. Patterns for fashioning perches from 240-cm boards. Make saw cuts as shown by the dashed lines.

against, and watch perch
choice through
your binoculars. Tally
in Table 4.1 the behavior
of the several species.
Each landing counts as one
record. If a bird lands on
one perch, then flies directly to one of another height,
count them both. We
want to investigate the
choice of perch height
when it is not complicated by social behavior, so watch carefully,
and tally a choice only when all four perches are bare of other
birds. Every several hours, move the perches to another location
within the same habitat type and repeat the procedure. In this way
you can build a summary record characteristic of each species and
not just one or a few individuals.

After you have several dozen records for each of several species,
you are ready to evaluate the hypothesis. Find the row total for
each species in Table 4.1. Divide this number into that species'
tally for each perch height and multiply by 100 to find percentage
use of each height. Add your calculated percentages to Table 4.2.
The species you studied may have differed greatly in their
responses to the different perch heights. For instance, Eastern
Meadowlarks may have landed 96% of the time on the 210-cm
perch, while Grasshopper Sparrows used the 90-cm perch 89% of
the time. Results such as these would clearly support the hypothesis that preferred perch height differs among species living
together in the same habitat. However, it is quite possible that
your results will not be so clear-cut. If Eastern Meadowlarks used
the 210-cm poles 52% of the time and 39% of Grasshopper
Sparrow landings were on 90-cm stakes, we might not be quite so
sure whether a real difference existed between species or whether

your results reflected chance variation, like flipping a coin four times and producing four heads instead of the expected two heads and two tails. You may wish to pursue the statistical analysis outlined below to decide more firmly whether real differences in perch choice existed among your species.

There is an intriguing refinement of this hypothesis about choice of perch height. Suppose we assume that grassland birds use perches for two separate purposes, to scan their territories for intruders of the same species, and to advertise their own presence by singing. A higher perch might allow better song transmission to the surrounding area, but it could also make the singer more vulnerable to predation from hawks since it would be farther from protective cover. These ideas suggest the hypothesis that birds perched high are there to sing and birds perched low are there to scan, but not to sing. We could predict that for any species, the percentage of birds perched high that sing would be much greater than the percentage of low perchers that sing, but we would have to deal with a major problem. Only males sing, and in most grassland species the sexes cannot be distinguished in the field. Since they do not sing, females might always use low perches, making our prediction appear to be true even if males sang equally from high and low perches. Short of color-marking individuals of known sex, a procedure beyond the scope of this book, there are two ways around this obstacle. One method is to examine the hypothesis in upland populations of the Red-winged Blackbird or in one of the few other grassland birds with distinguishable sexes. The other technique involves working only in habitats where vegetation is sparse or low enough that one individual bird can be followed visually while it is on the ground. Western Meadowlarks in short-grass prairie come to mind as one possibility. Here, you could identify an individual as a male after hearing it sing, then watch it for a lengthy period, recording the extent of its singing on high and low perches within its territory.

Statistical analysis.

The null hypothesis says that there is no difference in preferred perch height among species of grassland birds. The alternative hypothesis states that these species are partial to perch sites of different height. Appendix 1 contains a description of the Chi-square (χ^2) Test of Heterogeneity, and works through a sample analysis using some imaginary choices of perch height by grassland birds. Enter your observed numbers of landings, not percentages, in Table 4.3, then follow the methods of Appendix 1 to calculate expected values and the χ^2 statistic. By comparing your calculated χ^2 with the value in Table A1.2, you can decide whether to reject the null or alternative hypothesis at the 5% level of confidence. Degrees of freedom will equal the number of rows minus one, times the number of columns minus one; df = (r-1)(c-1).

Here, we are concerned with differences between species, and use the Chi-square Test of Heterogeneity. We could also test the hypothesis that any particular species has some preferred perch height. Methods would be the same as those used in the last chapter on excavation height in Downy Woodpeckers, and the Chi-square Test of Goodness of Fit would be the proper analysis. In this case, what would the null hypothesis and alternative hypothesis state?

Further reading.

Castrale, J. S. 1983. Selection of song perches by sagebrush-grassland birds. *Wilson Bulletin* **95**:647-655.

Harrison, K. G. 1977. Perch height selection of grassland birds. *Wilson Bulletin* **89**:486-487.

Zimmerman, J. 1971. The territory and its density dependent effect in *Spiza americana*. *Auk* **88**:591-612.

Table 4.1. Tally of perch heights selected by grassland birds

Species name	Number of landings				
	30-cm perch	90-cm perch	150-cm perch	120-cm perch	Row total
1					
2					
3					
4					

Table 4.2. Percentage of landings on four perch heights by grassland birds

| Species name | Percent of total landings | | | | |
	30-cm perch	90-cm perch	150-cm perch	120-cm perch	Row total
1					
2					
3					
4					

Table 4.3. Values needed to compare the preferred perch heights of grassland birds using the χ^2 test of heterogeneity

Species	Landings on 30-cm perch	Landings on 90-cm perch	Landings on 150-cm perch	Landings on 210-cm perch	Row total
1	Observed / Expected	Observed / Expected	Observed / Expected	Observed / Expected	
2	Observed / Expected	Observed / Expected	Observed / Expected	Observed / Expected	

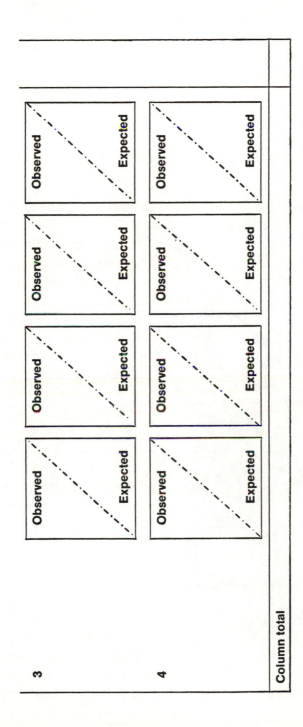

5

Do Northern Orioles Tend to Nest Over Water?

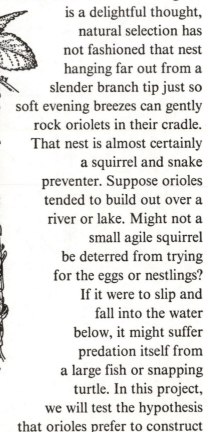

DO YOU SHARE my suspicion that Northern Orioles tend to build their basket nests over water? Although it is a delightful thought, natural selection has not fashioned that nest hanging far out from a slender branch tip just so soft evening breezes can gently rock oriolets in their cradle. That nest is almost certainly a squirrel and snake preventer. Suppose orioles tended to build out over a river or lake. Might not a small agile squirrel be deterred from trying for the eggs or nestlings? If it were to slip and fall into the water below, it might suffer predation itself from a large fish or snapping turtle. In this project, we will test the hypothesis that orioles prefer to construct their nests out over water. We can predict from our hypothesis that in cases where a tree stands on a river bank or lake shore, such that part of its canopy rises over land and part juts out over the water, any oriole nest it contains should hang over the water. Stated more formally, the percentage of oriole nests over water should be much greater than the percentage of canopy over water.

This a project for the autumn. After the leaves have fallen, scout along shorelines for oriole nests. These almost always hang from the outer "shell" of trees, and this gives us a way to evaluate our prediction. For each tree containing a nest, we need to estimate the total circumference of the outermost canopy, and the percentage of the total circumference over water.

Figure 5.1 is an schematic overhead view of a tree growing on a river bank. Practice walking along a measuring tape until each of your paces equals 1 m (39 inches). If you have hip boots, do not mind cold water, or if the stream or lake has frozen over, you can simply pace around the canopy margin to determine the total circumference and the length of the canopy margin over water.

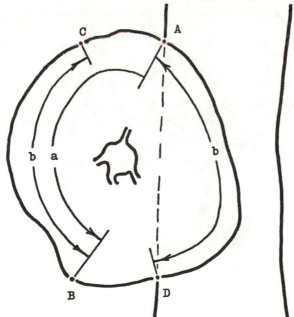

Fig. 5.1. Overhead view of a tree on a river bank, showing how to estimate canopy lengths.

Otherwise, follow the technique illustrated in Figure 5.1. Stand on the river bank under the canopy margin at point A, and locate point B where an imaginary line through the middle of the tree trunk crosses the far edge of the canopy. Then pace around under the landward side of the canopy edge from A to B, distance *a* in Figure 5.1. You now have half the number of paces for the circumference. Number of paces from A to B times 2 will give you the tree canopy's circumference in meters, assuming 1 m per pace. To find the length of the canopy over water, first pace from D to B. Then pace the same distance inward from point A and locate point C. The number of paces from C to B, distance *b*, is the length in meters of the canopy edge hanging over water. As you accumulate values for each waterside tree with an oriole nest, fill

in Table 5.1. Find the percentage of canopy length over water by dividing the total circumference of the canopy into the length of canopy over water, and multiplying by 100. Add this percentage to Table 5.1 for each tree.

If the individuals of a population of orioles prefer to nest over water, we would predict the percentage of nests over water to be much greater than the average percent canopy edge over water. The percentage of nests over water is determined by dividing the total number of nests you found into the number of nests hanging over water, and multiplying by 100. To find the average percent canopy edge over water, add together the percent canopy over water values for all trees, then divide by the number of trees. How do your two percentages compare? You may wish to evaluate more fully whether orioles prefer to have water under their nests by following the statistical analysis proposed at the end of this chapter.

Do you think that orioles might mistake black-topped roads for rivers? Perhaps you have noticed that a great many oriole nests seem to be constructed so they hang over a road, particularly a black-topped road. This impression may simply result from our detecting more nests on the side of trees under which we drive. It does seem possible, though, that if orioles tend to nest over water, they could "mistake" black-topped roads for rivers. If this were true, we would predict that the percentage of nests over black-top would be greater than the percent canopy edge over black-top. You can test this prediction using the same methods as you did for the waterside trees. Since gravel, dirt or cement roads might not mimic the appearance of rivers to the extent black-top does, we might expect no nesting preference for canopy overhanging them. What do your results show?

Statistical analysis.

The null hypothesis states that orioles have no tendency to build their nests over water. Our alternative hypothesis holds that they do tend to nest over water. If the null hypothesis is correct, then the percentage of nests over water and the average canopy length over water should be the same. If the alternative hypothesis is true, then the percentage of nests over water should be significantly greater than the average percent canopy length over water. We can use the Chi-square Test of Goodness of Fit described in Appendix 1 to test these predictions. It is not allowable to employ percentages in Chi-square tests because percentage is a continuous variable, so we must use the actual numbers of nests counted. Fill in your observed numbers of nests in Table 5.2. A brief calculation will give us the expected values. If the null hypothesis is correct, we would expect the number of nests over water to be proportional to the percentage of canopy edge over water. Multiply the average percent canopy over water, taken from the bottom of Table 5.1, times the total number of nests, and divide by 100. This result is the expected number of nests over water under the null hypothesis and should be entered in Table 5.2. Now go ahead and calculate the χ^2 as shown in Appendix 1; degrees of freedom equal one. Does the size of your χ^2 tell you to reject the null or alternative hypothesis?

Further reading.

Graf, R. L. and F. Greeley. 1976. The nesting site of the Northern Oriole in Amherst, Massachusetts. *Wilson Bulletin* **88**:359-360.

Schaffer, V. H. 1976. Geographic variation in the placement and structure of oriole nests. *Condor* **78**:443-448.

Table 5.1. Records for waterside trees containing nests of Northern Orioles

Tree number	Total circumference of canopy (m)	Length of canopy over water (m)	Percentage of canopy length over water	Position of nest (land or water)
1				
2				
3				
4				
5				
6				
7				
8				
9				
10				
11				
12				
13				
14				
15				
17				
18				
19				
20				

Average %
canopy over
water

= _____

% nests
over
water

= _____

Table 5.2. Nest location of Northern Orioles

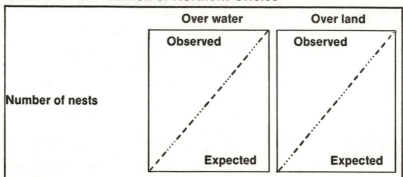

6

How Does a Robin Look for Worms?

IMAGINE that newly-arrived American Robins are running about your backyard in a gentle April rain. Every so often, one spots a half-hidden night-crawler, grabs it and begins the well-known tug of war. (Is the robin pulling as hard as it can, or just hard enough to extract the worm without breaking it? This is a problem for a mechanical

engineer as it involves the tensile strength of worms, and so on.) Our robin prizes out the worm and gobbles it down, but is still hungry. What should it do next? Should it turn to some random direction and run some random distance before stopping to look for worms again, or can it do better than that? Does it have some hunting strategy?

Suppose worms vulnerable to robins are not scattered about your yard at random. Maybe the soil is looser in some spots than in others, and has attracted more worms. Let's assume the grass cover is approximately uniform so the robins cannot tell this. Can the bird improve its chances for success anyway? We can construct a hypothesis which states that robins improve their catch by searching more carefully in the immediate area of a stop that produces a worm than in areas around stops that are unfruitful. Two of the ways a robin could restrict its search area after catching a worm can be stated as predictions. (1) After a stop producing a worm a robin runs a shorter distance before stopping again than after a stop not producing a worm. (2) The angle between runs separated by a stop producing a worm is smaller than the angle between runs separated by an unsuccessful stop. Fig. 6.1 illustrates how these two predicted tactics could work separately and in concert to keep a robin in the vicinity of its last meal. A robin decreasing both the length of runs and the angle

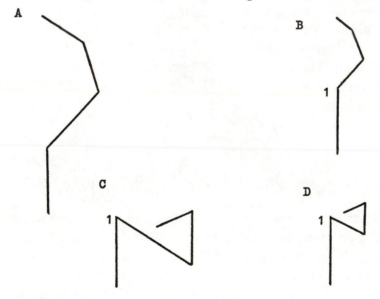

Fig. 6.1. Methods robins could use to remain close to a location where they had caught a worm. Part **A** shows stops and runs when no worms are caught. In section **B**, after catching a worm at location 1, the robin halves the length of each subsequent run, but keeps the angles between runs the same as in **A**. In **C**, after catching a worm at location 1, the robin halves the angles between runs, but keeps the lengths of runs the same as in **A**. Finally, in part **D**, after catching a worm at 1, the robin halves the length of each run and also halves the angle between runs.

between runs, as in part D of Fig. 6.1, has the best chance of remaining close to where it caught a worm.

Do robins support the hypothesis? Find a good high vantage point such as a hillside, second story window or comfortable tree branch overlooking a mown lawn. Pick out a robin and watch its runs and angles with reference to whether they follow the capture of a worm. In this procedure, we will assume that all the robins in your area have the same hunting behavior, so you can lump records from different birds. Our initial test will deal with just the first run after or not after a worm has been caught. A robin is about 21 cm long, so use the bird's own length to help you estimate run length in centimeters. To measure the angle between runs, you will have to remember the direction of the pre-stop run for comparison with the direction of the post-stop run; a compass may help your estimations. The angle between runs can vary between 180° when the robin goes straight ahead and 0° when the robin exactly backtracks. Try to obtain a large number of records for both the worm and no-worm categories, and add them to Tables 6.1 and 6.2. The average run length after a successful stop is found by adding up all the values in that column and dividing by the total number of values, 20 if you have filled in the column. Determine the other average values in the same way. Now, if the average run lengths and angles are a great deal smaller after a worm than when no worm has been caught, we have failed to disprove our hypothesis. If the averages are close together, we are not so certain because any difference may have been due to chance. You can resolve such ambiguous results by doing the statistical analysis suggested below.

Other hypotheses about how robins hunt are also testable. For example, the more removed a run is from the last worm, the longer it will be and the greater will be its angle with the last run. The larger the worm, the shorter the succeeding run and the smaller its angle with the run just prior to the worm.

Statistical analysis.

Appendix 1 explains the use of the Median Test to help decide between null and alternative hypotheses. Run-length in robins serves as the illustrative example. You can apply the Median Test to your records for run length and angle between runs by filling out Tables 6.3 and 6.4, then following the directions in Appendix 1.

Further reading.

Eiserer, L. A. 1980. Effects of grass length and mowing on foraging behavior of the American Robin (*Turdus migratorius*). *Auk* 97:576-580.

Smith, J. N. M. 1974. The food searching behaviour of two European thrushes: I. Description and analysis of search paths. *Behaviour* 48:276-302.

Table 6.1. Length of runs by worm-hunting robins

Length of run after a successful stop		Length of run after an unsuccessful stop	
Record number	Length (cm)	Record number	Length (cm)
1		1	
2		2	
3		3	
4		4	
5		5	
6		6	
7		7	
8		8	
9		9	
10		10	
11		11	
12		12	
13		13	
14		14	
15		15	
16		16	
17		17	
18		18	
10		19	
20		20	
Average length =		Average length =	

Table 6.2. Angle between runs of worm-hunting robins

Angle between runs separated by a successful stop		Angle between runs separated by an unsuccessful stop	
Record number	Angle (degrees)	Record number	Angle (degrees)
1		1	
2		2	
3		3	
4		4	
5		5	
6		6	
7		7	
8		8	
9		9	
10		10	
11		11	
12		12	
13		13	
14		14	
15		15	
16		16	
17		17	
18		18	
19		19	
20		20	

Average angle = _____   Average angle = _____

Table 6.3. Observed and expected run lengths of worm-hunting robins

	Runs after worm	Runs not after worm	Row total
Number of runs longer than or equal to the common median	Observed / Expected	Observed / Expected	
Number of runs shorter than the common median	Observed / Expected	Observed / Expected	
Column total			

Table 6.4. Observed and expected angles between runs of worm-hunting robins

	Angles after worm	Angles not after worm	Row total
Number of angles greater than or equal to the common median	Observed ⟋ Expected	Observed ⟋ Expected	
Number of angles smaller than the common median	Observed ⟋ Expected	Observed ⟋ Expected	
Column total			

7

When Do Great Blue Herons Give Up?

THE HUNTING STRATEGY of Great Blue Herons might best be termed the "mobile ambush." In almost any habitat containing sufficient frogs, fishes, or other prey, this largest of our herons may be seen poised along the water's edge or wading out to its feather-bottoms, searching the water. Periodically, the neck is cocked into the familiar S shape, then the rapier bill is launched to grasp the victim. Careful attention will show you that a heron does not stand for very long in one place. After watching intently, but in vain, for awhile, the bird will take one or several steps before becoming stationary again. How does it decide how long to wait in one place before moving? Put another way, what determines its giving-up time?

Suppose herons have to learn when to give up hunting in any one particular place. One very useful piece of information could be the average time interval between arriving at a hunting site and catching a fish or some other prey there. If herons can make such a calculation,

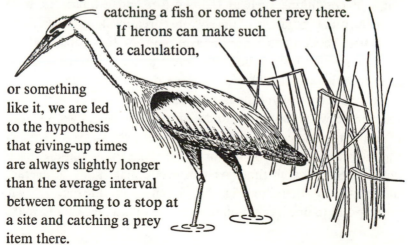

or something like it, we are led to the hypothesis that giving-up times are always slightly longer than the average interval between coming to a stop at a site and catching a prey item there.

Great Blue Herons hunt over a wide range of habitats and under a variety of climatic conditions. We find them in swamps and marshes, along the shores of lakes, and wading about in estuaries and shallow bays of the ocean. They are hardy birds and can be seen fishing in snowstorms as well as during high summer. This great spread of times and places gives us a way to test our hypothesis. We can predict that time to a catch will vary greatly over the species' range, but if we measure time to a catch in any particular location, we should always find it slightly less than giving-up time. Stated another way, catch time and giving-up time should be positively correlated; the longer the time to a catch, the longer the giving-up time.

This project requires taking records over the course of the annual cycle and in as many habitats as possible. You will need a stopwatch, notebook and binoculars.

Two kinds of records are needed, the number of seconds that a heron remains at each stop when it fails to catch prey, and the number of seconds between coming to a stop and catching a food item. For our study, we want to treat one habitat on one day as a single record. Do this by filling out a table in your notebook similar to Table 7.1. You will need to make a new table for each day and each habitat. Include in each table the location, date, and climatic conditions such as temperature, an estimate of wind velocity, and percentage of the sky obscured by cloud cover. After each field session, calculate the average time to a catch and the average giving-up time. Before you can proceed further, you will need to build up, say, 20 to 30 of these pairs of averages.

To evaluate our hypothesis, we want to see whether there is any relation between catch time and giving-up time. If, over a spread of habitats and seasons, the two numbers get larger or smaller together, this would support our hypothesis that giving-up time is determined by catch time. As you accumulate pairs of average numbers, add them to Fig. 7.1. Each point in Fig. 7.1 will correspond to one habitat on one day. It might be easier to make your own figure using graph paper, and you may have to if you find average catch times or giving-up times longer than those in Fig. 7.1.

Fig. 7.1 is called a scattergram. You can inspect yours as a method for assessing the hypothesis. First, though, we will make up some results to see what they can tell us. In Fig. 7.2A, I have added to the scattergram 25 points taken from various imaginary habitats on 25 days. As we look over these results, we see there is a close correspondence between the two values. It is clear that as average catch time increases, so does average giving-up time. These presumed results would certainly support our hypothesis that catch time determines giving-up time. Another imaginary set of 25 records is plotted in Fig. 7.2B. In this case, we look in

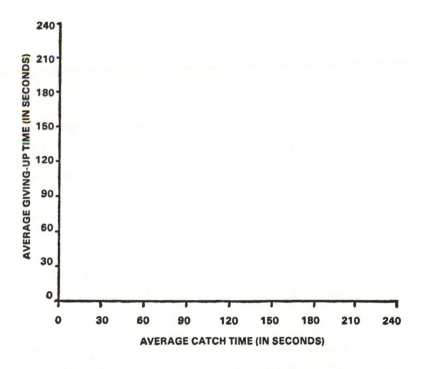

Fig. 7.1. **Observed** catch times and giving-up times of Great Blue Herons.

vain for any relationship. Giving-up time appears to be independent of catch time. For example, in Fig. 7.2B, catch times from 30
to 110 seconds can all correspond to a giving-up time of 60
seconds. From results such as these, we would reject our hypothesis; how long a heron hunts in one place is not determined by
its average catch time in that habitat on that day. It is very likely
that when you graph your own results, they will have a look
intermediate between the appearances of Figs. 7.2A and 7.2B.
Perhaps your curiosity will be sufficiently piqued that you will
work through the statistical analysis described below. By doing so,
you can make a firm decision about the validity of our hypothesis.

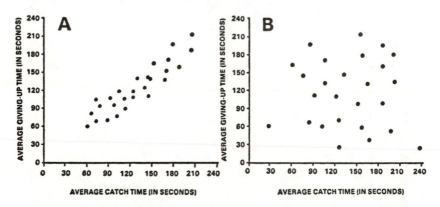

Fig. 7.2 Hypothetical catch times and giving-up times in Great Blue Herons
which support (**A**) and fail to support (**B**) our hypothesis

The methods of this project are directly applicable to a large
number of species that hunt using the mobile ambush strategy.
The hypothetical relationship between catch time and giving-up
time can be tested in other herons, flycatchers, kingfishers, hawks,
bluebirds and shrikes. Maybe you can think of other possibilities.

Statistical analysis.

Let's consider some numbers which illustrate the troublesome
sort of intermediate results produced by many field studies.
Examine the 25 points in Fig. 7.3. It looks like there might be a

relationship between catch time and giving-up time, but it is not very clear-cut, and the apparent relationship could simply be due to chance variation in the herons' behavior. We really cannot decide whether catch time determines giving-up time without performing a statistical test. When we want to know if two quantities vary together in some predictable way, we do what is called a *correlation analysis.*

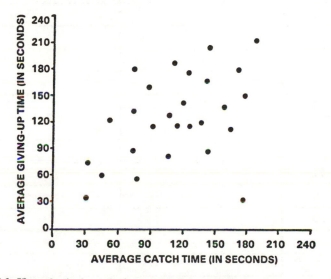

Fig. 7.3. **Hypothetical** catch times and giving-up times of Great Blue Herons yielding intermediate results

Appendix 2 presents the Spearman Rank Correlation Analysis, and uses hunting behavior of Great Blue Herons as an illustrative example. Try this correlation analysis, using Table 7.2 to arrange your numbers.

Further reading.

Betts, B. J. and D. L. Betts. 1977. The relation of hunting site changes to hunting success in Green Herons and Green Kingfishers. *Condor* **79**:269-271.

Recher, H. F. and J. A. Recher. 1969. Comparative foraging efficiency of adult and immature Little Blue Herons *(Florida caerulea). Animal Behaviour* **17**: 320-322.

Table 7.1. Catch times and giving-up times of Great Blue Herons in one place on one day

Record number	Time to a catch (in seconds)	Giving-up time (in seconds)
1		
2		
3		
4		
5		
6		
7		
8		
9		
10		
11		
12		
13		
14		
15		
16		
17		
18		
19		
20		

Average
catch
time

= _____

Average
giving-up
time

= _____

Table 7.2. Numbers needed to analyze the correlation between catch time and giving-up time using the Spearman Rank Correlation Test

Habitat and/or day	Average catch time	Average giving-up time	Rank of average catch time	Rank of average giving-up time	Difference between ranks	Difference between ranks squared
1						
2						
3						
4						
5						
6						
7						
8						
9						
10						
11						
12						
13						
14						
15						
16						
17						
18						
19						
20						

Σ Diff. = 0 Σ Diff.^{2}

= _____

8

Can Turkey Vultures Smell Their Way to Food?

IT IS OFTEN HELD that birds have a very poor sense of smell. While this assertion is probably true generally, there appear to be a few exceptions. Some of the more primitive species have well-developed olfactory lobes in their brains, large olfactory nerves, and functioning olfactory tissues in their nasal passages. During the last few decades, a small number of such species have been shown experimentally to behave as if they possessed a functioning sense of smell. Anatomically, Turkey Vultures have very good noses. Why? We know that vultures feed on carrion, and we know that carrion is at least noticeable to the human nose. Combining these pieces of information, we create the hypothesis that a sense of smell is useful to Turkey Vultures because it increases their ability to find food. From this hypothesis we predict that a piece of carrion with an odor strongly apparent to the human nose will attract Turkey Vultures even when it is hidden from sight. If it does not have a strong odor, hidden carrion will not attract Turkey Vultures. To test this

prediction, we need a large field, two small piles of brush, and two quantities of carrion, one unripe and one very ripe.

52

Start this project by gathering some freshly killed animal remains. Fish would do nicely. Road kills such as woodchucks would be excellent. Divide this material and place each half in a large plastic bag. Leave one bag outside in a sunny location where its contents can ferment nicely, and store the second bag in your freezer. Check the outdoor bag periodically over the next several days. When it has developed a sufficient aroma, you are ready to test the prediction. The night before the test day, remove the second bag from the freezer so its contents will be thawed. Alternatively, the fresh material could be obtained on the day of the experiment, so a freezer would not be necessary. Take both bags to an open location frequented by vultures, such as a large field. Gather grasses, stems, or branches into two piles large enough to conceal the carrion from sight. The two brush piles should be at least 100 m apart on a line perpendicular to wind direction, as shown in Fig. 8.1. Toss a coin to decide which brush

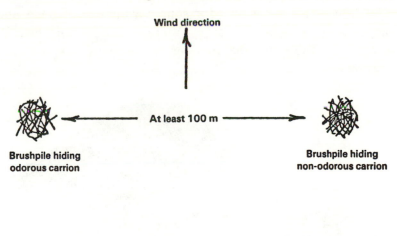

Fig. 8.1. Relationships of brushpiles hiding carrion with the observation point, wind direction, and each other.

pile gets which kind of carrion, then dump the contents of each bag on the ground and cover them thoroughly with the brush. Before starting the test, place the empty odorous bag inside the non-odorous one and tie it securely so no extraneous odors will confound the experiment. Retreat upwind to your observation point. This should be as far away as possible so your presence will not unduly affect the vultures' behavior. Ideally, you could use an automobile as a blind and watch events through binoculars.

If Turkey Vultures find carrion by smell, they should follow an airborne odor trail by flying upwind to its source. This gives us two kinds of behavior we can use to compare responses to odorous and non-odorous brushpiles. First, a vulture following an odor trail should fly upwind and then, after passing the odor source, should turn and fall off with the wind for some distance before again flying up the odor trail. Use Table 8.1 to tally the number of individual flights upwind to each brushpile. Second, after flying near a hidden odor source a number of times and pinpointing its location, Turkey Vultures should land near it. Record in Table 8.2 the number of landings next to each brushpile.

If you tally a large number of flights and landings near the odorous carrion and few or none near the non-odorous carcass when both are hidden from sight, you can conclude that Turkey Vultures use a sense of smell to find food. Those with access to Black Vultures as well as Turkey Vultures have a nice opportunity to compare olfactory prowess in the two species, both of which subsist largely on carrion. Do you find a large discrepancy between the responses of the two species?

Statistical analysis.

The null hypothesis would predict no difference in the number of flights to or landings near the two brushpiles. Use Tables 8.3 and 8.4 and the Chi square Test of Goodness of Fit described in Appendix 1 to make your evaluation. Expected values for the odorous and non-odorous brushpiles will be identical. Degrees of freedom will equal one in both tests.

Further reading.

Bang, B. G. and S. Cobb. 1968. The size of the olfactory bulb in 108 species of birds. *Auk* **85**:55-61.

Stager, K. E. 1967. Avian olfaction. *American Zoologist* **7**:415-419.

Table 8.1. Tally of upwind flights of Turkey Vultures to odorous and non-odorous hidden carrion

	To odorous brushpile	To non-odorous brushpile
Tally of flights		

Table 8.2. Tally of landings of Turkey Vultures near odorous and non-odorous hidden carrion

	Near odorous brushpile	Near non-odorous brushpile
Tally of landings		

Table 8.3. Observed and expected flights upwind toward odorous and non-odorous hidden carrion

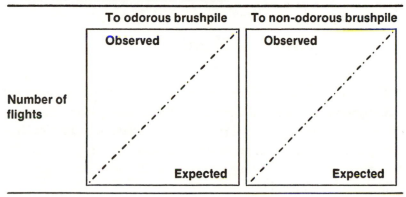

Table 8.4. Observed and expected landings near odorous and non-odorous hidden carrion

9

Why Do Ospreys Hover?

THANKS largely to hard work by a small band of visionary conservationists, the Osprey is flying back from oblivion. Where it was once decimated by pesticide residues, particularly along the Atlantic coast and throughout the Great Lakes region, this elegant fisherman is again building ungainly stick nests on utility poles and dead snags.

What a pleasure it is to watch this bird wheel to and fro, quartering a shallow bay with its head cocked sharply downward, it eyes seldom leaving the water below. Periodically, we see the great stoop and splash as the Osprey often follows its talons completely under water. Upon struggling back into the air, it invariably shakes the water from its plumage in mid-flight like some feathered seadog. After a successful dive, Ospreys presumably reduce their flight drag by pointing their fish head-first in the talons, just as World War II torpedo bombers carried their "fish."

Where their habitat permits, Ospreys usually hunt from a perch, sitting quietly on the top of some old snag along the shoreline, monitoring the water below for prey movement. In order to see fish far out from shore though, Ospreys must hunt on the wing.

Most of their aerial hunting is done while alternately flapping and gliding, but periodically a bird will pull up into a stall and remain stationary in the air column by beating its wings quite strenuously. Such exertion requires much more energy than flapping or gliding, which leads to the question, why do Ospreys hover. Why should hovering be a better hunting strategy than simply diving directly from gliding flight? One could hypothesize that hovering is used because it increases the chances of catching prey. If this were true, we would predict that more dives from hovers than from gliding flight result in a catch.

Take up a station overlooking some large bay or estuary. As Ospreys glide, hover, and dive, record whether each dive commenced from hovering or from gliding-flapping flight. From now on, we will call the latter category of flight an interhover. Try to watch a number of different birds so you can be assured that your findings are characteristic of the entire local population. As you proceed, fill in Table 9.1. Then summarize your records by totalling the entries within each column and adding your results to Table 9.2. Calculate the percentage of dives from a hover that resulted in a fish by dividing the total number of dives from hovers into the number of dives from hovers that were successful, and multiplying the result by 100. Do the same calculation for dives from interhovers. If the percent success of dives from hovers is much greater, you might conclude that Ospreys hover because this technique promotes fishing efficiency. If the two percentages are about equal, you might decide to reject the hypothesis.

In certain parts of the country, while doing this project, you might have the great good fortune to see the aerial marvel of a Bald Eagle pirating your poor study animal's catch in mid-air.

A number of other birds hunt from hovers and interhovers Belted Kingfishers, American Kestrels, and Rough-legged Hawks, for example, could be used in place of Ospreys to evaluate the question, why hover. The kestrel and hawk would test your ingenuity because their "hovering" is sometimes a complex stairstep pattern of sequential hovers as they drop lower to the ground before pouncing on prey. As a first approach, you might consider each entire stairstep sequence to be a single hover.

Statistical analysis.

Use of a statistical procedure can help decide whether to reject the null hypothesis or alternative hypothesis. The Chi-square Test of Heterogeneity is appropriate for this project. Following the directions in Appendix 1, find the row and column totals in Table 9.3, derive the expected values, and calculate the χ^2 statistic. Be sure to take a large sample size so all your expected values will be greater than five. Degrees of freedom will equal one.

Further reading.

Dunstan, T. C. 1974. Feeding activities of Ospreys in Minnesota. *Wilson Bulletin* **86**:74-76.
Grubb, T. C., Jr. 1977. Why Ospreys hover. *Wilson Bulletin* **89**:149-150.

Table 9.1. Success of Osprey dives from hovers and interhovers

Record number	Dive from a hover	Dive from an interhover	Successful	Not successful
1				
2				
3				
4				
5				
6				
7				
8				
9				
10				
11				
12				
13				
14				
15				
16				
17				
18				
19				
20				
21				
22				
23				
24				
25				
26				
27				
28				
29				
30				

Table 9.2. Summary of Osprey fishing success from a hover or interhover

	Dives from a hover	Dives from an interhover
Number of successful dives		
Number of unsuccessful dives		

Table 9.3. Observed and expected outcomes of Osprey dives from hovers and interhovers

	Dives from a hover	Dives from an interhover	Row total
Number of successful dives	Observed / Expected	Observed / Expected	
Number of unsuccessful dives	Observed / Expected	Observed / Expected	
Column total			

10

How Refined is a Hummingbird's Palate?

HUMMINGBIRDS leave a vivid impression. How can anything that dainty and beautiful be so fearless, and even feisty? Because they are so small and their hovering flight so strenuous, hummingbirds use energy very rapidly. It is not surprising that one of their major sources of food is the nectar of flowers. The sugar in nectar is an excellent source of calories, and its dissolved condition means it quickly passes out of the gut and into the hummingbird. However, a large proportion of nectar is water, which has no caloric value, but must be lugged around anyway by the hummingbird. We know that different species of flowers, and even the same flower at different times, contain differing sugar concentrations. It should be advantageous for hummingbirds to focus their feeding on flowers with high sugar content. To do this, they must be able to tell high from low sugar concentrations. Can they, and if so, with what precision? Here, we will try to find out. Our first hypothesis says that hummingbirds select nectar on the basis of sugar concentration. The second hypothesis states that below some threshold difference in sugar concentration, hummingbirds become indiscriminant between nectar sources. You will need a box of Domino brand "Hostess Sugar Tablets," a cylinder or other measuring device graduated in milliliters (ml), and two commercial hummingbird feeders. The Domino brand sugar tablets I have in mind are those commonly found in restaurants; they measure 8 × 20 × 28 mm (millimeters). Many garden centers carry hummingbird feeders, as do a number of mail order supply houses, one of which is Duncraft, Penacook, New Hampshire 03303.

Each sugar tablet is 4.9 g (grams) of pure sucrose. With this information, we can mix up sugar solutions of several concentrations and test our hypotheses. Table 10.1 details the relationship between number of tablets dissolved in one liter (l) (a liter = 1,000 ml) of water and the resulting sugar concentration. Dissolve 5 tablets in one l to make a 2.4% solution, then make a 29.4% solution by stirring 60 tablets into another liter of water. Add sufficient red food coloring to make each solution bright red; this is the common color of "hummingbird flowers" and will act as an initial attractant for the hummers. After filling one feeder with each of the solutions, hang them 1 m apart in a location frequented by hummingbirds. Label each feeder with its sugar concentration. Over the next several days, replenish the two solutions as needed, and toss a coin to determine the position of the feeders daily so the birds will not come to associate a particular sugar concentration with a particular feeder location.

Now you are ready to test the first hypothesis. Early each morning for the next 15 days, fill up the two feeders and determine the position of each by coin toss. Allow the birds to use them throughout the day. Late in the afternoon, perhaps when you arrive home from school or work, measure the volume of solution in each feeder by pouring the solution into your graduated cylinder. Record these values in Table 10.2. Pour the solutions back into the feeder and position them in the same location where they had been hanging all day. Let hummingbirds use the two feeders for one hour. Then measure the volume left in each feeder and record these values in Table 10.2. At the end of the 15-day period, determine the average volume of each concentration consumed per hour. If the average volume of 29.4% solution consumed per hour was much larger than the average for the 2.4% solution, you have supported the hypothesis

that hummingbirds select flowers based on the sugar concentration of nectar.

Our second hypothesis postulated a threshold difference in concentration between nectar sources, below which hummingbird discrimination fails. Let's assume you found a large difference in response to the 2.4% and 29.4% solutions. We can predict that as the more dilute concentration approaches closer and closer to 29.4%, at some point the preference for the 29.4% feeder will disappear. In straightforward fashion, we can run through a series of 15-day experiments comparing the response to the 29.4% solution with responses to 4.9% through 27.0% solutions. Simply replace the 2.4% solution with each of the others in turn, and proceed. As you increase the concentration of the more dilute solution in this stepwise fashion, at some point the average consumptions per hour at the two feeders may suddenly become about equal. Such a result would be evidence for a threshold percentage difference in concentration. You could conclude that the hummingbirds of the species you studied cannot tell apart two sugar concentrations differing by that percentage, or less. However, it is possible you will not get such a sharp change in behavior. Maybe the preference for the stronger solution diminishes gradually rather than suddenly. When does a real choice between feeders cease, and only a chance difference remain? By performing a series of Median Tests, as explained in the section on statistical analysis at the end of this chapter, you can reach a firm conclusion about whether a threshold is present and where it is.

We have looked for a threshold difference from 29.4% sugar, but the location of the threshold could depend on concentration. Maybe if one solution is very concentrated, say 49% sugar, the threshold difference is smaller. Can you design a series of experiments evaluating how threshold difference might be sensitive to solute concentration?

Statistical analysis.

The null hypothesis states that hummingbirds do not select nectar based on sugar concentration. One alternative hypothesis says they do discriminate, and the second alternative states that they can discriminate only if sugar concentrations are further apart than some threshold difference. We can test these premises with Median Tests, as explained in Appendix 1. Start with your results from the initial comparison of 2.4% and 29.4% solutions. Find the common median volume the birds drank from both feeders over 15 days. Then fill in Table 10.3, calculate expected values, and determine the χ^2 value. If your χ^2 value is larger than that in Table A1.2, you reject the null hypothesis. How do we look for the threshold difference? Simply repeat the analysis for each successively closer pair of concentrations, 4.9% and 29.4%, 7.4% and 29.4%, and so on. The second alternative hypothesis predicts that sooner or later as you compare responses to 29.4% and another concentration increasingly close to it, your calculated χ^2 will drop below tabulated χ^2, indicating no difference in responses to the two feeders at the 5% level of confidence. Copy the format of Table 10.3 into your notebook, substituting another concentration for 2.4%, and rework the Median Test until you find a χ^2 value smaller than the tabulated one. You could then conclude you have discovered the threshold difference, or a concentration difference very close to it since we did use 5% increments of our solute concentrations.

Further reading.

Stiles, F. G. 1976. Taste preferences, color preferences, and flower choice in hummingbirds. *Condor* 78:10-26.
Van Riper, W. 1958. Hummingbird feeding preferences. *Auk* 75:100-101.

Table 10.1. Relationship between number of sugar tablets dissolved in 1 liter of water and the percent sugar concentration of the solution

Number of Hostess Sugar tablets per liter	Percent sugar concentration
5	2.4
10	4.9
15	7.4
20	9.8
25	12.2
30	14.7
35	17.2
40	19.6
45	22.0
50	24.5
55	27.0
60	29.4
65	31.8
70	34.3
75	36.8
80	39.2
85	41.6
90	44.1
95	46.6
100	49.0

Table 10.2. Volumes of 2.4% and 29.4% sugar solutions used by hummingbirds

Day	Initial volume of 2.4% solution (ml)	Final volume of 2.4% solution (ml)	Volume of 2.4% solution used in one hour (ml)	Initial volume of 29.4% solution (ml)	Final volume of 29.4% solution (ml)	Volume of 29.4% solution used in one hour (ml)
1						
2						
3						
4						
5						
6						
7						
8						
9						
10						
11						
12						
13						
14						
15						
			Average volume per hour = _____			Average volume per hour = _____

Table 10.3. Observed and expected volumes of two sugar solutions used by hummingbirds

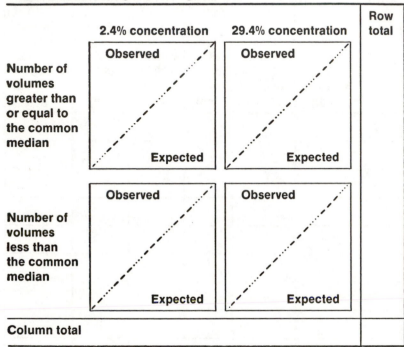

11

Can Birds Divide Energy by Seconds?

URING the early days of television, some quiz shows
featured a prize category in which contestants were given all
the food they could collect from a supermarket in 5 minutes.
When the bell sounded, did they rush up and down the aisles
throwing items into their shopping baskets at random? Not a
chance. They made straight for the beef counter. Why? The best
strategy for these prize winners, measured in dollars per minute,
was to concentrate on the beef. The contestants had a common
currency which they used to compare beef with all the items in the
store that they could have collected during the 5-minute prize
period. One of the major areas of current interest in field
ornithology concerns whether birds looking for food behave as
the contest winners did. We will investigate how efficiently birds
can select food items.

One hypothesis currently being analyzed states that birds
should choose food types giving them the best ratio of energy
intake to "handling time." To do this they must be able to divide
the energy content of any food item by the length of time it takes
them to find and eat that item. The food type providing the largest
ratio should be preferred. Parts of this hypothesis are rather
complicated and are covered elsewhere (see Further reading at the
end of this chapter), but we can test the essence of the idea in an
experiment with mealworms and a winter bird feeder.

Suppose a Carolina Chickadee has the choice of eating a large mealworm or a small one. Should it prefer to concentrate on just one size? Current theory would say yes, the chickadee should always take the worm size giving it the larger amount of energy per unit of handling time. Notice, the hypothesis does not necessarily predict that the larger worm should be preferred; the one with the higher ratio of energy per handling time should be.

For the project, you will need several hundred mealworms, which may be purchased at almost any pet store. Larger quantities of mealworms delivered airmail on reasonable terms can be obtained from Rainbow Mealworms, Inc., P.O. Box 4525, Compton, California 90220. Keep them in a refrigerator or some other cool place. For several days before you start the project, replace the other food on your feeder periodically with mealworms so the birds will learn to recognize them as food.

Your mealworms will come in a variety of sizes, and we will take advantage of this variation. Dump a containerful of mealworms onto a dish and sort them by length to the nearest millimeter. You will find they squirm around less as you hold a ruler alongside if they are cold, so pop unmeasured worms back into the refrigerator periodically, or do the whole job outside in cold weather.

You should now have several dozen mealworms of each length between 15 and 20 mm sorted into different containers. The first thing we want to know is the birds' handling time for mealworms of each length. I will concentrate on the 15 mm and 20 mm worms from now on, but you can easily expand the project to include intermediate-length worms. I will also confine my attention to chickadees, but the experiment can be applied to any of several other birds that take mealworms from feeders.

Clear off the feeder and pile just the 15-mm worms in the center. Chickadees will soon start carrying off the worms, one at a time, to a nearby tree or shrub where they will hold them under their feet and use their bills to tear them apart to eat. We will consider handling time to be the number of seconds between starting to eat and finishing a mealworm. Using a stopwatch, make 10 handling time observations for the 15-mm worms and enter the results in Table 11.1. Replace the remaining 15-mm worms with a pile of 20-mm worms and repeat the procedure. Then calculate the average handling time for each worm size and enter these values at the bottom of Table 11.1.

Next, we need to know the energy content of each size mealworm. Current scientific practice uses the Joule as the unit of energy, but we will retain the more familiar calorie (= 4.17 Joules). From Table 11.2, which lists the energy content of mealworms of various lengths, we can see that the values for 15-mm and 20-mm worms are 158 calories and 355 calories, respectively.

We want to know the ratio of energy content to handling time in our two worm sizes. Although you will want to use your own results, let's assume the chickadees' average handling times are 20 seconds for 15-mm worms and 60 seconds for 20-mm worms. The ratios of energy content to handling time would then be 158/20 = 7.9 calories per second for 15-mm worms, and 355/60 = 5.9 calories per second for 20-mm worms.

If the hypothesis that chickadees use this ratio to select food items efficiently is correct, we would predict that given a choice between 15-mm and 20-mm worms, they should prefer the 15-mm length. This prediction is easily tested. Place piles of 15-mm and 20-mm worms about 30 cm apart on your feeder. Tally in Table 11.3 the worm sizes chosen by the chickadees. Did the birds prefer the length with the larger energy/handling time ratio? If the preference was weak, you might wish to use the statistical analysis at the end of this chapter to see if chance variation alone could have been responsible.

A number of other questions could be explored with these methods. For example, how discriminating are the chickadees? Do they choose, say, between 17-mm and 18-mm mealworms on the basis of the energy/handling time ratio? Tufted Titmice also carry off and eat one mealworm at a time, but titmice are a good deal larger than chickadees and therefore have a shorter handling time for any given worm size. How do their choices of mealworm size compare with those of chickadees? White-breasted Nuthatches often gobble down whole mealworms right on the feeder. Since their handling times are essentially zero, do they always choose the larger of two mealworm sizes?

Statistical analysis.

The null hypothesis says choice of mealworm size is not a function of energy/handling time. The alternative hypothesis predicts that chickadees will always choose the mealworm size with the greater energy/handling time ratio. If the chickadees selected one worm size in most, but not all cases, you can determine whether your result could have been due to chance alone by using the Chi-square Goodness of Fit Test described in Appendix 1. To find the values expected under the null hypothesis of no choice, divide the total number of worms taken by two. Degrees of freedom equals one, and both expected values must be at least five. Use Table 11.4 to arrange your numbers for the test.

Further reading.

Krebs, J. R., J. T. Erichsen, M. I. Webber and E. L. Charnov. 1977. Optimal prey selection in the Great Tit *(Parus major)*. *Animal Behaviour* 25:30-38
Wolf, L. L. 1975. Energy intake and expenditure in a nectar-feeding sunbird. *Ecology* 56:92-104.

Table 11.1. Handling times, in seconds, for chickadees eating mealworms of two lengths

Record number	Handling time for 15-mm mealworms	Handling time for 20-mm mealworms
1		
2		
3		
4		
5		
6		
7		
8		
9		
10		

Average = _____ Average = _____

Table 11.2. Length and energy content of mealworms

Length (in millimeters)	Energy content (in calories)
13	79
14	118
15	158
16	197
17	237
18	276
19	315
20	355
21	394
22	434
23	473
24	513
25	552

Table 11.3. Tally of the number of each worm size chosen by chickadees

	15-mm mealworms	20-mm mealworms
Tally		

Table 11.4. Observed and expected choice of mealworms by chickadees

	Mealworm length with smaller energy/handling time ratio	Mealworm length with greater energy/handling time ratio	Row total
Number of mealworms eaten	Observed / Expected	Observed / Expected	

12

Why do Cattle Egrets Associate With Cattle?

NORTH AMERICAN Cattle Egrets have a predilection for large grazing animals. Their partiality evolved in Africa and accompanied the species' invasion of the New World earlier this century.

Why the attraction to cattle? Possibly, cattle could furnish the egrets protection from predators if hawks, foxes, and such were reluctant to venture near large animals. Here, we will focus on the hypothetical feeding advantage to be gained around large grazers. The main foods of Cattle Egrets are grasshoppers and other field-dwelling insects. Many of these prey species are camouflaged to match the vegetation, which could make them difficult for egrets to discover. As a cow slowly grazes across a pasture, she moves her head to and fro while cropping grass. Thus, she could be serving as a grasshopper flusher for the egrets near her. Insects jumping or flying from the cow's path would become visible to the egrets and vulnerable to capture. On any rangeland or pasture at any one time, some Cattle Egrets may be seen in close company with cattle while others look for food away from the ungulates. This duality of behavior enables us to form a prediction. If Cattle Egrets forage near cows because insects are easier to find there, then birds near cattle should catch more insects per unit time than those hunting by themselves. It is not

78

difficult to tell when an egret has caught an insect because it always jerks back its head in a very distinctive manner when swallowing. We will assume that each head jerk equals one captured insect.

Station yourself overlooking a pasture that contains both cattle-following and non-cattle-following egrets. Using binoculars and stopwatch, pick one egret and count the number of its head-jerk swallows during a 5-minute period. Then record the same information for an egret of the other category. Continue this pattern until you have 25 records

each for birds foraging near cattle and away from cattle in the same pasture. Enter your numbers in Table 12.1, and then calculate the average insects/5 minutes for each group. If the cattle-following group generated a much greater number, you have supported the hypothesis that egrets stay with cows because their foraging efficiency increases there. The statistical analysis provided below will allow you to conclude whether the observed difference could have occurred simply as a chance outcome, or whether there was a real, non-random difference in feeding efficiencies.

Remember the other notion about egrets staying near cows for protection from predators? The protection hypothesis would predict that cattle standing still should be as attractive to egrets as cattle actively grazing. Is this prediction true? You can increase your certainty with the Chi-square Goodness of Fit Test described in Appendix 1.

Many birds appear to make their food easier to find by following various animate or inanimate objects moving through their habitat. You can use the methods described here to investigate such cases. For example, why do American Kestrels sometimes follow grain combines, American Crows follow plows, American Wigeons follow American Coots, Starlings follow hogs, Brown-headed Cowbirds follow cattle, and Laughing Gulls follow Brown Pelicans?

Statistical analysis.

The alternative hypothesis predicts that egrets near cows catch more food per unit time than do those foraging away from cattle. The null hypothesis claims there is no difference. Performing the Median Test outlined in Appendix 1 will let you decide which hypothesis to reject at the 5% level of confidence. After calculating the common median, place your observed and expected results in Table 12.2, then proceed with the analysis.

Further reading.

Grubb, T. C., Jr. 1976. Adaptiveness of foraging in the Cattle Egret. *Wilson Bulletin* **88**:145-148.

Smith, S. M. 1971. The relationship of grazing cattle to foraging rates in anis. *Auk* **86** 876-880.

Table 12.1. Numbers of insects caught during 5 minutes by Cattle Egrets foraging next to cattle or away from cattle

Record number	Insects per 5 minutes near cattle	Insects per 5 minutes away from cattle
1		
2		
3		
4		
5		
6		
7		
8		
9		
10		
11		
12		
13		
14		
15		
16		
17		
18		
19		
20		
21		
22		
23		
24		
25		

Average = _____   Average = _____

Table 12.2. Observed and expected numbers of insects caught during 5-minute periods by Cattle Egrets

	Egrets near cows	Egrets away from cows	Row total
Number of catches greater than or equal to the common median	Observed / Expected	Observed / Expected	
Number of catches less than the common median	Observed / Expected	Observed / Expected	
Column total			

13

Do Male and Female
White-breasted Nuthatches
Look for Food in Different Places?

THE BIRDS OF WINTER woodlands spend most of their
waking hours looking for food. Over the last several decades,
many workers have reported that species living together forage in
different parts of the forest. Brown Creepers hitch their way up a
tree trunk searching bark crevices for insect eggs, larvae, and
adults, then fly to the base of a neighboring tree and repeat the
process. Woodpeckers probe and drill. Chickadees concentrate
their activity on twigs, and nuthatches spiral around trunks and
branches. In this fashion different species may divide up the food
resources of their habitat and, in doing so, reduce competition for
food enough so they can coexist. More recently, it has been
discovered that male and female
woodpeckers of some species look
for food differently, and current
thinking has it that such sex-
specific foraging has evolved
to promote coexistence of the
sexes of a species in the same area.

White-breasted Nuthatches
can also be sexed in the field.
After some practice with
binoculars, you should
be able to distinguish
the shiny, coal-black feathers
of the male's cap from the duller
charcoal-gray to gray crown of

83

the female. In this project, we will examine the hypothesis that male and female White-breasted Nuthatches look for food in different parts of the same woodland. Your first task is to practice sexing this species in the field. The best conditions occur on bright sunny days. For better viewing, try to approach your subjects with the sun behind you. After some experience, you should be able to identify the sex of most individuals, even under cloudy skies. A male and female White-breasted Nuthatch almost always forage close together as they move through the winter territory they defend against others of their species. This bit of natural history is useful. If you can sex one bird of the pair, you can assume the other bird is of the opposite sex.

There are a number of ways that male and female White-breasted Nuthatches could separate their food searching. We will examine two possibilities, set down as predictions. (1) Males and females look for food at different heights in the woodland. (2) The sexes search different branch sizes.

Walk slowly through the woods while scanning for nuthatches. You will find most pairs by homing in on their call notes. Be sure to locate both male and female. By taking foraging records of both birds at the same time, you can eliminate complications resulting from variation in weather conditions or other factors. When you have both sexes pinpointed, record in Table 13.1 the estimated height above the ground and the estimated trunk or branch diameter where each bird is foraging. We will want information from several pairs. Allow at least 1 minute between successive records from a single pair, and do not take more than five records in a row at any one time on the behavior of the same pair. Be careful to exclude cases where either bird is resting or preening. Both must be foraging. After you have a number of records, which may take several study sessions to accumulate, calculate the average height and average substrate diameter for each sex and enter these numbers at the bottom of Table 13.1. If there is a large difference between the sexes in average height or branch size, you have supported the hypothesis that White-breasted Nuthatches do have sex-specific foraging behavior. If the two sexes differ by only a few meters of height or a few centimeters of branch diameter, this could be due to a chance outcome. In such a case, you could decide on the likelihood of chance being responsible by following the statistical analyses at the end of this project.

Your results will be particularly interesting because there appears to be geographical or habitat-induced variation in White-breasted Nuthatch foraging. We know that in a ponderosa pine forest in Colorado, females of this species foraged higher in trees and on smaller branches than males did. In a deciduous woodland in Ohio, the two sexes used the same heights and branch sizes. Records from different parts of North America, and from deciduous and coniferous forest, may help resolve the present disparity.

This project has only been concerned with foraging differences between the sexes of one species. The same approach can be used to compare different species in the same woodland. Do Downy Woodpeckers forage higher in the trees than Hairy Woodpeckers do? Are the branches inspected by chickadees smaller than those searched by Tufted Titmice? Are the substrates used by kinglets even thinner? Other categories of foraging can be investigated. Species or sexes can be compared in their use of various substrate types. For instance, are the proportions of sightings on trunk, branch, log, vine, shrub, and ground different? Do male and female woodpeckers peer-and-poke, scale bark, or excavate holes to the same extent? Do male White-breasted Nuthatches move upward on trees more than females do, or vice versa?

Statistical analysis.

Our null hypothesis states that male and female White-breasted Nuthatches do not differ in their foraging behavior. From the alternative hypothesis, which says they do differ, we derived two predictions, both of which can be assessed with the Median Test. Following directions in Appendix 1, add observed and expected values to Tables 13.2 and 13.3. Then proceed to determine whether the null hypothesis or the alternative hypothesis should be rejected at the 5% level of confidence. If you have been able to take paired records in every case, the sample sizes for males and females should be equal. In both tests, degrees of freedom will equal one.

Further reading.

Grubb, T. C., Jr. 1982. On sex-specific foraging behavior in the White-breasted Nuthatch. *Journal of Field Ornithology* **53**:305-314.

Williams, J. B. 1980. Intersexual niche partitioning in Downy Woodpeckers. *Wilson Bulletin* **92**:439-451.

Willson, M. F. 1970. Foraging behavior of some winter birds in deciduous woods. *Condor* **72**:169-174.

Table 13.1. Records of foraging in White-breasted Nuthatches

Record number	Male height (meters)	Female height (meters)	Male substrate diameter (centimeters)	Female substrate diameter (centimeters)
1				
2				
3				
4				
5				
6				
7				
8				
9				
10				
11				
12				
13				
14				
15				
17				
18				
19				
20				
21				
22				
23				
24				
25				

Averages

Table 13.2. Observed and expected foraging heights, in meters, of male and female White-breasted Nuthatches

	Male height	Female height	Row total
Number of records equal to or greater than the common median	Observed ⟋ Expected	Observed ⟋ Expected	
Number of records less than the common median	Observed ⟋ Expected	Observed ⟋ Expected	
Column total			

Table 13.3. Observed and expected substrate diameters, in centimeters, used by foraging male and female White-breasted Nuthatches

	Male substrate	Female substrate	Row total
Number of records equal to or greater than the common median	Observed ⟋ Expected	Observed ⟋ Expected	
Number of records less than the common median	Observed ⟋ Expected	Observed ⟋ Expected	
Column total			

14

Where Do White-breasted Nuthatches Cache Their Supplies?

BIRDS have two methods of storing excess food, larder hoarding and scatter hoarding. Larder-hoarding species gather dispersed food and bring it to one or a few concentration points. Acorn Woodpeckers are classic larder hoarders. The individuals of a clan gather acorns from an extensive area and store them in one or a few trees which are defended through the winter. Red-headed Woodpeckers do the same with acorns and beech nuts, but these birds are solitary in winter; each provisions and guards its own larder.

Much less is known about the storage techniques of scatter hoarders. These species have no central storage depot. Some birds like the Clark's Nutcracker and the Blue Jay deposit seeds throughout their home range in small packets. Others such as chickadees and nuthatches do the same with individual seeds or insects. In this project, we will explore the hoarding behavior of the White-breasted Nuthatch. One question we might ask is, where do these nuthatches deposit excess food. It seems safe to conclude that natural selection has favored hoarding in species whose habitats undergo periodic food shortages. We then would

90

expect birds to use up the stored food during hard times. This leads to the hypothesis that White-breasted Nuthatches store food during times of plenty in the same parts of their habitat where they forage during lean days. For instance, nuthatches plucking beech seeds from newly-opened pods in October should disperse them throughout their territory in places they will be using during the upcoming winter. We can test our hypothesis by comparing cache sites with the foraging records for male and female White-breasted Nuthatches you gathered while working through Chapter 13. Either project can be done first, but you will want to use the same woods for both.

If your woodland has an abundance of seed-bearing trees, record the behavior of nut-hatches storing this natural crop. But if your area is in a floodplain forest or some other seed-poor habitat, you will have to furnish a super-abundant resource. Purchase a 60-cm length of galvanized stovepipe or heating duct 15 cm in diameter. Cut out a hole 3 cm in diameter so that its edge is 1 cm from one end of the pipe. Then fasten a board to the same end of the pipe so it extends 15 cm beyond the hole, as shown in Fig. 14.1. Punch a small hole in the other end of the pipe on the side opposite the 3-cm opening. Finally, make a cover for the pipe from a coffee can lid or some other piece of metal. Squirrels will chew through a

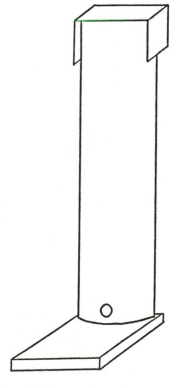

Fig. 1. A feeder made from stovepipe or heating duct.

plastic or wooden lid. Fill the stovepipe with sunflower seeds. Then drive a nail into a tree 1.5 to 2 m from the ground, hang the feeder on it, and slide on the metal cover. This large capacity feeder will hold enough seeds so you will need to refill it only weekly or even less often. After placing the feeder in your woods in late autumn, scatter several dozen seeds on the board to help your birds find the supply.

When nuthatches have found the seeds and are busy scatter hoarding them, you are ready to test the hypothesis. Each time a nuthatch removes a seed, use your binoculars to watch its subsequent behavior carefully. If it flies to another tree, wedges the seed into a bark crevice, then hammers it open ("hatches" it) and eats it, omit the record. We are only interested in cases where the bird wedges the seed into a crack and then leaves. Each time you observe such unambiguous caching behavior, enter in Table 14.1 the height above ground and the branch diameter of the seed's position. When you have several dozen records, calculate the average height and the average substrate diameter where each sex stored seeds and enter these numbers at the bottom of Table 14.1. If the average storage heights and substrate diameters are very similar to the average foraging heights and substrates in Table 13.1, you may wish to conclude that nuthatches scatter-hoard food items in late autumn among sites where winter foraging will discover them. Since it is exceedingly unlikely that your storing and foraging averages will be identical, there may be some doubt in your mind whether the two results are really the same, or whether only a chance similarity is responsible. You can decide more confidently by performing the statistical analysis described at the end of this chapter.

Major opportunities exist for the study of scatter hoarding. For example, how far from its source will hoarders scatter their food? How close together are caches placed? How rapidly are hoards used up during times of scarcity? How much of its surplus does a hoarder lose to other birds? What is the "shelf-life" of food in the cache? Answers to questions like these have direct bearing on an understanding of why scatter-hoarding has evolved. Can you convert some of these questions into hypotheses and then test them?

Statistical analysis.

The null hypothesis predicts that there is no difference between foraging and hoarding height or substrate size. The alternative hypothesis claims the two types of behavior involve different heights and substrate diameters. Both predictions can be examined with the Median Test detailed in Appendix 1. Use Tables 14.2 and 14.3 to organize your results for male nuthatches; construct similar tables in your notebook for the females. For each sex, determine whether the null hypothesis or alternative hypothesis should be rejected at the 5% level of confidence. All two-sample Median Tests, such as these, have one degree of freedom. The Median Test can also be used to test whether male and female nuthatches have different storing behavior. What would be the null and alternative hypotheses? Which one do you reject?

Further reading.

Kilham, L. 1974. Covering of stores by White-breasted and Red-breasted Nuthatches. *Condor* 76:108-109.

Tomback, D. F. 1980. How nutcrackers find their seed stores. *Condor 82*:10-19.

Table 14.1. Records of scatter hoarding in White-breasted Nuthatches

Record number	Height where male stored seed (m)	Height where female stored seed (m)	Substrate diameter where male stored seed (cm)	Substrate diameter where female stored seed (cm)
1				
2				
3				
4				
5				
6				
7				
8				
9				
10				
11				
12				
13				
14				
15				
16				
17				
18				
19				
20				
21				
22				
23				
24				
25				

Averages

Table 14.2. Observed and expected hoarding and foraging heights of male White-breasted Nuthatches

	Hoarding height	Foraging height	Row total
Number of records equal to or greater than the common median	Observed ⟋ Expected	Observed ⟋ Expected	
Number of records less than the common median	Observed ⟋ Expected	Observed ⟋ Expected	
Column total			

Table 14.3. Observed and expected hoarding and foraging substrate diameters of male White-breasted Nuthatches

	Hoarding substrate diameter	Foraging substrate diameter	Row total
Number of records equal to or greater than the common median	Observed — Expected	Observed — Expected	
Number of records less than the common median	Observed — Expected	Observed — Expected	
Column total			

15

What Determines Individual Distance?

HAVE YOU been struck by the uniform spacing of swallows resting on a telephone wire? It almost seems as if the birds measure the interval between where they alight and where their nearest neighbors are perching. Quite a few species show this spacing characteristic which is called *individual distance*, a rather precisely defined zone of intolerance to approach by conspecifics. Here we will evaluate the hypothesis that individual distance is determined by the reach of a perched bird, that conspecifics are not permitted inside the distance a resting bird can reach with its bill.

Numerous species congregate along linear perch sites. They range from the large gulls and cormorants loafing on a seawall or boathouse ridgeline to species as small as Bank Swallows resting on utility lines near their nesting colonies. This large variation in body size gives us material for a prediction. Since large birds can reach out farther with their bills, if our hypothesis is correct, there should be a positive correlation between body size and individual distance. The bigger the bird, the farther from its neighbors it perches or stands.

97

Begin this project by unrolling a spool of adhesive tape and sticking it to your kitchen floor or some other smooth clean surface. Using a ruler as a guide, blacken alternating 1-cm-wide bands with a waterproof-ink marking pen. After the ink has dried, reroll the tape onto the spool.

Locate sites where birds of several different body sizes congregate in linear formations. Besides the possibilities mentioned above, Starlings sitting on fences around feedlots, doves perched on the sides of stock tanks, and House Sparrows resting on your clothesline come to mind. You may have other examples in your area. Unroll your tape and apply it on or just below and parallel to the surface the birds are using. If your birds appear unwilling to land on or just above the white-and-black tape, you can color the white bands a light brown to make them less conspicuous. Even then, it may be necessary to leave the tape in place for several days before your birds become accustomed to its presence.

After the birds are again perching nicely in a line on or just above the tape, you are ready to begin taking notes. Retreat some distance from the tape so you can view the perching line at an approximately perpendicular angle through binoculars or tele scope. For each species, take 10 records of body width and 10 records of what appear to be minimum stable distances between adjacent birds. Use outermost body plumage as the end points for both measurements. List your results in Table 15.1. Then calculate the average body width and average minimum individual distance for each species, and add these to the table.

Now evaluate the prediction that individual distance is a positive function of body size. For each species, you have a pair of numbers, average body width and average minimum distance between neighbors, both taken to the nearest centimeter. Mark in Fig. 15.1 the point corresponding to each pair of numbers. Are all the points arranged in a narrow band from lower left to upper right in the figure? If so, you have have proven the prediction and failed to reject the alternative hypothesis. It is quite possible that

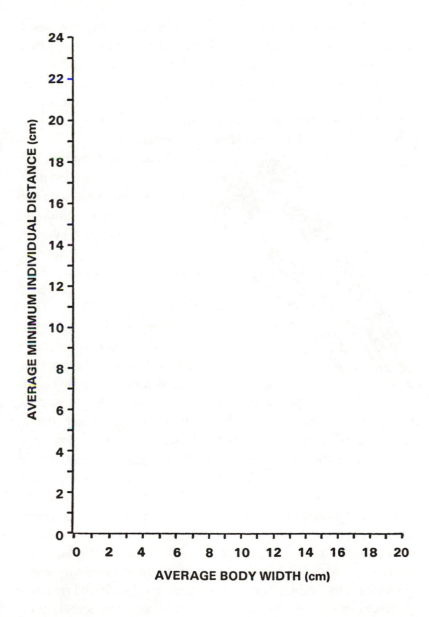

Fig. 15.1. Body size and individual distance.

your points are not so neatly arranged. Maybe they are in a broad band rather than a narrow one. Here, we are in doubt whether there really is a relation between body size and individual distance, or whether the weak correlation we see is just a product of random chance. To help you make a firm pronouncement on the hypothesis, you might wish to analyze your results statistically in the fashion detailed at the close of this chapter.

Individual distance has been studied only slightly and there are opportunities for investigating a number of questions. For example, a few species are known to dispense with individual distance in very cold weather, with birds then huddling in contact with each other, presumably to keep warmer. What is the threshold temperature at which individual distance breaks down? Just after youngsters have fledged, they often sit next to their parents at loafing sites. Is the individual distance between parent and offspring smaller than the species average? Sometimes larger and smaller species intermingle. When neighbors differ in size, is the distance between them set by the larger bird, the smaller one, or is it some compromise distance? When individuals of the same species perch next to one another, is the distance between them larger when they face the same way than when they face opposite directions? If it is, can you formulate an explanatory hypothesis? We need a general hypothesis to explain why some species have individual distances while others do not and routinely perch in bodily contact. Deserts have very substantial fluctuations between day and night temperatures. Could it be that desert birds have thin plumage to keep cool during the day, and perch together in contact to stay warm at night?

Statistical analysis.

The null hypothesis states that body size is not related to individual distance. The alternative hypothesis predicts a positive correlation between bird width and minimum individual distance. You can decide whether to reject the null hypothesis or the alternative hypothesis at the 5% level of confidence by testing your findings with the Spearman Rank Correlation Test explained in Appendix 2. Arrange your records in Table 15.2, then determine Spearman's r.

Further reading.

Beal, K. G. 1978. Temperature-dependent reduction of individual distance in captive House Sparrows. *Auk* 95:195-196.

Grubb, T. C., Jr. 1973. Absence of "individual distance" in the Tree Swallow during adverse weather. *Auk* 90:432-433.

Grubb, T. C., Jr. 1974. Individual distance in the Herring Gull. *Auk* 91: 637-639.

Table 15.1. Body width and individual distance, measured to the nearest centimeter

Record number	Body width	Individual distance	Record number	Body width	Individual distance
Species:			Species:		
1			1		
2			2		
3			3		
4			4		
5			5		
6			6		
7			7		
8			8		
9			9		
10			10		
Averages			Averages		
Record number	Body width	Individual distance	Record number	Body width	Individual distance
Species:			Species:		
1			1		
2			2		
3			3		
4			4		
5			5		
6			6		
7			7		
8			8		
9			9		
10			10		
Averages			Averages		

Table 15.1. Body width and individual distance, measured to the nearest centimeter (continued)

Record number	Body width	Individual distance	Record number	Body width	Individual distance
Species:			Species:		
1			1		
2			2		
3			3		
4			4		
5			5		
6			6		
7			7		
8			8		
9			9		
10			10		
Averages			Averages		

Record number	Body width	Individual distance	Record number	Body width	Individual distance
Species:			Species:		
1			1		
2			2		
3			3		
4			4		
5			5		
6			6		
7			7		
8			8		
9			9		
10			10		
Averages			Averages		

Table 15.2. Numbers needed to analyze the correlation between body width and individual distance using the Spearman Rank Correlation Test

Species	Average body width	Average minimum individual distance	Rank of average body width	Rank of average minimum individual distance	Difference between ranks	Difference between ranks squared
1						
2						
3						
4						
5						
6						
7						
8						

$\sum$ Diff. = $\sum$ Diff.² =

16

Is the Bigger Bird Always the Bully?

THE IDEA that animal societies possess hierarchies of social dominance was first supported in domestic chickens several decades ago, and it has since been demonstrated in a number of species of wild birds. The dominant animal supplants the subordinate from food sites, roost sites, and so on, and wins any fights that arise when the eventual subordinate does not defer soon enough. We now know that both intraspecific (within-species) dominance and interspecific (between-species) dominance occur in nature. Studying intraspecific dominance generally requires color-banding or otherwise marking animals so they can be individually recognized. Here, we will concentrate our attention on dominance relationships between species, and between sexes of the same species where plumage differences allow the sexes to be distinguished.

We want to investigate the hypothesis that interspecific and intersexual social dominance status is a consequence of body size; the larger bird is always dominant. Species coming to feeders in the winter will serve as study animals. Use two large square boards as feeders. Place one on the ground and one approximately 1 m off the ground on a post. More birds will use the feeders if they are positioned near trees and shrubbery. Although there is some overlap, most winter species can be labelled as either ground feeders or tree feeders. We will want to assess dominance relations within each feeding group.

You have often seen one bird supplant or displace a second bird from its position on your feeder. We will use these supplantings as a measure of dominance; the supplanter is dominant and the supplanted individual is subordinate. Supplanting attacks can be encouraged by concentrating the food source. Nail a small container such as the lid from a peanut butter jar to the middle of each of your feeders. Generally, only one bird at a time will feed from such a point source, so supplantings should occur frequently. Add to the containers the usual kinds of seed mixtures and suet. As you accumulate records of supplanting attacks, stop every 15 minutes or so and return to the container any seeds that the birds have scattered over the feeder.

Our hypothesis predicts that a larger bird should always supplant a smaller bird, never the reverse. We can test this prediction by first recording our results in what is called a *dominance matrix*. Write down the names of all the species that routinely use your feeders, separating the sexes in species where they are visually discernable. Then use Table 16.1 to determine the weight of each bird species and/or sex. M.H. Clench and R.C. Leberman of the Carnegie Museum of Natural History collected most of these weights in western Pennsylvania. While the weights of your birds could vary somewhat from those in the table, the relative sizes of different bird types should be about the same. Arrange your bird types and their weights in a dominance matrix such as the one shown in Table 16.2. You can either construct separate dominance matrices for the ground foragers and tree foragers, or block out one large matrix combining both categories.

Now begin to fill in your matrix by placing tally marks in the appropriate boxes. Particularly on very cold days, when all the birds are hungry, you should be kept quite busy. In such weather, interrupt your study periodically and spread out the seed for 10 or 15 minutes so the smaller birds will have a good chance to eat. After you have collected a few hundred records, which may require several study sessions, you can evaluate our hypothesis. Examine each pair of bird types in your matrix, for example, Tufted Titmouse and Carolina Chickadee, or female Red-bellied Woodpecker and male Downy Woodpecker. In Table 16.3,

record
the
difference
between
their weights
and which bird type is dominant. Also, calculate the percentage of all records in which the larger type dominated, and enter that result in the right-hand column of Table 16.3. If all percentages on the right of Table 16.3 are 100%, or close to it, you could conclude that our hypothesis seems correct, that social dominance is a positive function of body size. However, if you run into complications trying to interpret your results, you may need to construct new hypotheses. Suppose female White-breasted Nuthatches are dominant to Tufted Titmice. Can you create a hypothesis to explain why? Suppose you find that as the difference in weights between any two bird types gets smaller, the percentage of supplantings dominated by the larger bird drops away from 100%. Can you determine a threshold percent weight difference and predict that a larger bird will invariably dominate a smaller one only when they differ in weight by more than the threshold percent?

Two kinds of dominance hierarchies are thought to exist. In a *peck-right hierarchy*, dominance status is absolute; the dominant individual is always dominant. In a *peck-dominance hierarchy*, one individual is usually dominant, but reversals of status can occur. Sort through your pairs of bird types and locate the peck-dominance relationships. In some of these pairs, you may find that one bird type supplanted another bird type not much more than 50% of the time. Do these cases show a real dominant-subordinate relationship, or could your outcome have been just due to random chance? You can get a much better idea by working through the following statistical procedure.

Statistical analysis.

Suppose you work out the dominance relations for male and female House Sparrows and you find that males supplant females 27 times and females supplant males 12 times. A null hypothesis would state that there is no difference in dominance status between the sexes, and that your result was just due to random chance. An alternative hypothesis would maintain that your results show males dominating females in a peck-dominance hierarchy. We can decide whether to reject the null or alternative hypothesis by employing the Chi Test of Goodness of Fit detailed in Appendix 1. Under the null hypothesis, we would expect equal numbers of supplantings by males and females. In the example here, the total number of observed supplantings was 39, so our expected number of supplantings employed in the χ^2 procedure would be 19.5 for both male and female sparrows. Referring to your own results, determine whether your suspected peck-dominance pairings could be due solely to chance. Degrees of freedom will be one in every case. Make sure to analyze only pairings for which both expected values are five or more.

Further reading.

Clench, M. H. and R. C. Leberman. 1978. Weights of 151 species of Pennsylvania birds analyzed by month, age and sex. *Bulletin of the Carnegie Museum of Natural History.* Number **5**.

Dixon, K. L. 1954. Some ecological relations of chickadees and titmice in central California. *Condor* **56**:113-124.

Recher, H. F. and J. A. Recher. 1969. Some aspects of the ecology of migrant shorebirds. II. Aggression. *Wilson Bulletin* **81**:140-154.

Table 16.1. Weights of birds likely to use bird feeders in winter[1]

Bird species		Weight (g)	Bird species		Weight (g)
Red-headed Woodpecker		73[2]	Field Sparrow		14
Red-bellied Woodpecker	♂	80	Fox Sparrow		37
	♀	74	Song Sparrow		25
Downy Woodpecker	♂	27	White-throated Sparrow		28
	♀	27	White-crowned Sparrow		28
Hairy Woodpecker	♂	70	Dark-eyed Junco		22
	♀	66	Red-winged Blackbird	♂	72
Common Flicker	♂	129		♀	45
	♀	127	Common Grackle	♂	118
Blue Jay		90[2]		♀	96
Black-capped Chickadee		11	Brown-headed Cowbird	♂	53
Carolina Chickadee		10		♀	40
Boreal Chickadee		10	Purple Finch	♂	25
Tufted Titmouse		22		♀	24
Red-breasted Nuthatch	♂	12	Common Redpoll	♂	15
	♀	11		♀	13
White-breasted Nuthatch	♂	22[2]	Pine Siskin		16
	♀	21	American Goldfinch	♂	15
Brown Creeper		9		♀	14
Starling		82	Evening Grosbeak	♂	62
Northern Cardinal	♂	52		♀	60
	♀	49	House Sparrow	♂	28
Tree Sparrow		19		♀	27

1. Almost all weights are taken from the monograph by Clench and Leberman listed under Further reading at the end of the chapter. The weights used are those available from the month closest to the middle of winter.
2. These weights are of birds in the collection of The Ohio State University Museum of Zoology.

Table 16.2. Sample dominance matrix of bird types using a winter feeder, and their weights in grams

	Supplanted individual					
Supplanter individual	Male Red-bellied Woodpecker 80	Female Red-bellied Woodpecker 74	Male Downy Woodpecker 27	Female Downy Woodpecker 27	Tufted Titmouse 22	Caroline Chickadee 10
Male Red-bellied Woodpecker 80						
Female Red-bellied Woodpecker 74						
Male Downy Woodpecker 27						
Female Downy Woodpecker 27						
Tufted Titmouse 22						
Carolina Chickadee 10						

Table 16.3. Paired dominance outcomes of larger and smaller birds using bird feeders

Larger bird type	Smaller bird type	Weight difference (in grams)	Number of supplantings by larger bird	Number of supplantings by smaller bird	Percent supplantings by larger bird

17

Is a Hungrier Bird a More Sociable Bird?

IN the woodlands of North America in winter, it is not unusual to find four or five different bird species moving together in a group as they glean their food from trees, ground and shrubs. These groups have been called *mixed-species foraging flocks*. Although nobody quite knows why they exist, two major features have been put forth to explain the evolution and maintenance of these mixed-species groups. (1) By foraging with other species and entering into a kind of mutual protection society with them via special warning calls, each bird decreases its chances of being caught unawares by a hawk. (2) The birds of each species notice when an individual of another species finds a food item. By copying the foraging behavior and location of successful fellow members of the flock, each bird increases its chances of finding food. The notion that mixed-species flocks occur in response to avian predators is very hard to analyze experimentally because keeping close tabs on the whereabouts of free-ranging accipitrine hawks is very difficult. (It might be accomplished if the accipiters were radio-tagged, a study that could be attempted. However, such an enterprise would involve equipment and money beyond this book's purview.) We will concentrate on the second suggestion. Reworded into a hypothesis, this states that birds join mixed-species flocks to increase their chances of finding food because they can mimic successful flock-mates of other species.

Over the course of the winter, the amount of food a bird needs per day varies with temperature. Birds are homeothermic animals, as we are, which means that regardless of air temperature, they maintain a constant high body temperature. If we want to keep our house at 22°C (72°F) in winter, then the colder the day, the more fuel we have to burn. So it is with birds. In colder weather,

112

they too must "burn more fuel." If birds can find more food in mixed-species flocks, and if they need more food in colder weather, then the colder the temperature in winter the more often they should forage with other species.

To test this prediction, find a large woods at some distance from the nearest bird feeder; we don't want the study birds' behavior affected by access to a supplemental food supply. As you walk through the woods, note the social inclinations of each bird you encounter. Classify individuals as foraging alone, with others of their species only (in a monospecific flock), or with birds of other species in a mixed flock. We want to be sure that each bird is actively attracted to other birds and is not just aggregating independently at some plentiful food supply such as the nuts on the ground under a beech tree. To guarantee that other birds are the attraction, consider a bird to be foraging socially only if you see it following or being followed by another bird. To test our hypothesis about the value of mixed-species flocking, we will lump birds foraging by themselves or with only conspecifics into a category called "otherwise." So, each bird must be foraging either in a mixed-species flock or otherwise. Our prediction says that there is an inverse relationship between temperature and occurrence of any species in a mixed flock: the colder the temperature the greater the percentage of individuals foraging with other species. The food needs of birds in winter should also be influenced by wind velocity and solar radiation. In order to make interpretation of your results less difficult, try to reduce the impact of these two factors by working on the project only when wind velocity is low and the sky is either clear or completely overcast, whichever is the more common in your area. As you encounter each individual, place in Table 17.1 the social environment in which it is foraging. Also note the air temperature by using a portable thermometer, and add that value to the same row in Table 17.1. Take only one record per individual before going on to other birds. You may later return to the same forager, but in the meantime it will have had a good chance to change its social behavior, so the records can be considered independent.

After you have 50 to 100 records of sociality for each common species, you can evaluate the hypothesis. For each species, group your records to the nearest 5°C and calculate the percentage of birds at that 5 degree interval which foraged in mixed-species groups. In your notebook, construct a scattergram for each species similar to the one in Fig. 17.1, and fill in the points corresponding to your pairs of numbers. If the points in your scattergrams are arranged in a narrow band from upper left to lower right, you can conclude that the species you are examining support the hypothesis that birds join mixed-species flocks to increase their chances of finding food. If the points in your figures are more scattered, their meaning may be more difficult to interpret, and you may wish to test the hypothesis by using the statistical analysis described at the end of this chapter.

This project centers on the value of mixed-species flocking. Another hypothesis might state that foraging with any other individuals, whether of the same or different species, increases the chances of finding food. You could test the prediction that the extent of solitary foraging is positively related to temperature, the higher the temperature, the greater the percentage of non-social birds.

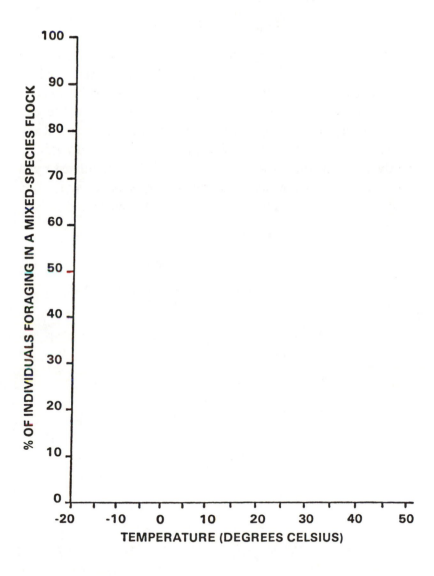

Fig. 17.1. Relation between ambient temperature and percentage of individuals of a species foraging in a mixed-species flock.

Statistical analysis.

The null hypothesis says that temperature has no relation to social behavior in winter birds. The alternative hypothesis predicts a negative correlation between temperature and the percentage of individuals of a species accompanying other species. We can evaluate these competing hypotheses with the Spearman Rank Correlation Test detailed in Appendix 2. A calculated r significantly larger, ignoring the negative sign, than the tabulated r will cause us to reject the null hypothesis. For each of your study species, arrange your values as in Table 17.2, then proceed.

Further reading.

Morse, D. H. 1970. Ecological aspects of some mixed-species foraging flocks of birds. *Ecological Monographs* **40**:119-168.
Smith, S. M. 1967. An ecological study of winter flocks of Black-capped and Chestnut-backed Chickadees. *Wilson Bulletin* **79**:200-207.

Table 17.1. Social environment of birds foraging in a winter woods, and accompanying temperature

Species	Number foraging in a mixed-species flock	Number foraging "otherwise"	Air temperature (degrees Celsius)
1			
2			
3			
4			
5			
6			
7			
8			
9			
10			
11			
12			
13			
14			
15			
17			
18			
19			
20			

Table 17.2. Numbers needed to analyze the correlation between the percentage of individuals of a species foraging in mixed-species flocks and air temperature using a Spearman Rank Correlation Test

Air temperature (°C)	Percent of individuals in mixed-species flocks	Rank of air temperature	Rank of percent in mixed-species flocks	Difference between ranks	Difference between ranks squared
-20					
-15					
-10					
-5					
0					
5					
10					
15					
20					

$$\sum \text{Diff.} = \underline{\hspace{2cm}} \qquad \sum \text{Diff.}^2 = \underline{\hspace{2cm}}$$

18

Do Next-door Neighbors
Have Non-aggression Pacts?

S UPPOSE you are a male Song Sparrow bustling about
your breeding territory in early spring. You have an ex-
hausting schedule of patrolling your kingdom, finding food, and
singing frequently to attract females and repel other males. You
dispute your boundary with a neighbor, bolt down an insect, belt
out a couple of songs from a perch in a hawthorne, rush over to
confront a strange male trespassing in your far corner by the alder
bush, on and on through the day. Every minute spent bickering
with your neighbors over boundaries means less time for attract-
ing females, and for foraging. Is there any way natural selection
could have equipped you to make your job more efficient, to help
you conserve time
and energy?
We know from
studies using
sophisticated
equipment that no
two males of the same
species have
precisely the same
songs. There are always at
least minor differences
in pitch and temporal patterning. Now suppose that you could
learn to recognize a song as belonging to Harry next door. You
needn't waste time and energy investigating, unless Harry were
singing in the middle of your own ground. An unfamiliar song

119

would be a different matter; you would have to rush over and drive out the stranger before he could establish himself on your territory. However, maybe Harry is your big problem. He is living next door, ideally situated to make a land grab at any minute. Maybe you had better keep him in his place and not be so concerned about some stranger who might be just passing through. Let's test these possibilities with real Song Sparrows.

Before we go further, a small digression about dialects is needed. We know that the males of any given population all have songs with roughly the same pitch and temporal patterning, and that these song types differ among populations. Such variations on the theme of a species' song have been called *populational dialects*, or just dialects. By listening to a tape-recording of a Song Sparrow, certain bird linguists can surmise where in North America it was made, just as you can place someone geographically according to whether he says "tire iron," "tar arn," or "tah ahn." From playback experiments with tape-recorded song, we know that both male and female songbirds can discriminate their own from unfamiliar dialects.

In this project, we want to know whether a male bird responds differently to a next door neighbor than to a bird from, say, a kilometer away when all three birds have the same dialect. One hypothesis states that male Song Sparrows are most aggressive in response to songs of immediate neighbors. The second model postulates the response as being greater to songs of strangers than to songs of neighbors. For this project, you will need a stopwatch, portable cassette tape-recorder with separate microphone, and three "endless loop" tape cassettes. These loops are a special variety of cassette normally used as part of telephone answering service equipment. There are several brands; Radio Shack carries a loop cassette (catalogue number 43-401), which has a playing time of 20 seconds. That is, every 20 seconds the loop starts playing the same sounds over again. Those with access to certain ancillary pieces of equipment such as parabolic microphone reflectors and remote speakers will know how to incorporate them into the following methods, but they are not necessary for the project.

The first thing we need to do is to locate a population of songbirds and determine territory boundaries. I will stay with Song Sparrows, but any of a large number of open-country or brushland species would be appropriate. You might consider combining this project with the study of song perch height in Chapter 4.

Construct a detailed map of the population's habitat, perhaps your block, a nearby park, or a brushy field near water. Record the location of trees, shrubs, laundry poles, buildings, swing sets, any perch from which a Song Sparrow might sing. Next, focus your attention on one individual male sparrow in the mapped area and follow his movements for several hours. Every time he lands, record the location on your map. Be very careful not to lose track of the bird so you can be confident that all the points on your map belong to the same individual. Here is a case where a co-worker would be very valuable; one of you could observe and one could record. As you proceed, use a special code, perhaps an "s," to denote every site where your bird engages in a bout of singing. After several hours, you will know the outer boundary of the bird's territory, the proportionate use of each part of the territory, and the bird's favorite singing perches. Now locate the male closest to the one you have just watched, and in similar fashion note where he lands and sings over the course of several hours. Finally, map the singing perches of a third bird far enough away so he is certainly out of earshot of the first two, perhaps a kilometer in the case of Song Sparrows.

We can now record the songs of these three birds, and we will want each loop cassette to have one song of one bird. Consult your mapped territories. For each male, find the most used perch within your reach. Tape the microphone close to the perch so it points toward where the bird habitually sits while singing. Place

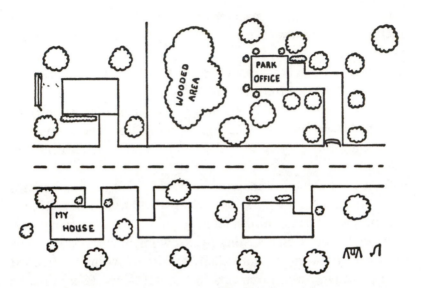

the recorder on the ground and connect the microphone wire. It
may take some time for the sparrow to habituate enough to the
presence of the microphone and recorder that he will resume
singing from the perch, and this can be a problem if your time for
the project is limited. You can avoid any undue time delay by
making dummy microphones and recorders. Roughly duplicate
the shape and color of your equipment out of scrap wire, wood,
cigar boxes and the like. Two or three days before the recording
date, place the three dummies near the predetermined song
perches. When you switch each dummy for the real article on
recording day, the singer should no longer be bashful about
cooperating. Once the recorder is in place, turn it on and retreat
the minimum distance required before the male will use the perch
to sing. The tape loop will be going around endlessly in the
"record" mode. Now let's suppose the bird flies to the perch and
starts a song bout, but at first he is facing away from the
microphone. Wait until he sings a full song close to and/or facing
the microphone. As soon as he finishes this song, rush from your
hiding place to the perch site and turn off the recorder. Assuming

that a Song Sparrow song lasts 4 seconds, you will have 16 seconds to reach the machine and turn it off. Don't worry about flushing the bird; he won't leave his territory. Now play back the loop. If it contains sounds other than the one song you want, time the length of the song in seconds with your stopwatch. Then retreat to a quiet place. Play the loop there and stop it precisely when the song ends. Subtract the length of the song from 20 seconds. Switch to the record mode, and let the tape run, while "recording" silence, for exactly the non-singing interval of the loop. For example, if you have previously recorded a song of 4 seconds duration, now "record" for precisely 16 seconds. This procedure will give you a tape loop which plays one full song, and nothing else, every 20 seconds. Using your other two tape loops, repeat this procedure for the next door neighbor and for the stranger a kilometer away.

We now have the pure records of neighbor and stranger songs needed to test the hypotheses. Locate on your map the boundary line between the two neighbors. Pick one of these two birds to test first, and choose a playback site approximately 10 m on his side of the boundary. We want to compare his responses to songs of neighbor and stranger coming from that point. Insert the "neighbor song" cassette into your tape-recorder, place the recorder on the ground at the playback site, turn it on at approximately natural volume, and quickly withdraw to an observation point. With the aid of your stopwatch, count the number of songs the territory holder sings within 5 minutes of the first song playback. Also, estimate the closest approach the territory holder makes to the recorder. Place these results for Bird 1 in Table 18.1. Turn off the recorder and remove it from the test site. Change to the "stranger song" cassette and, after allowing 30 minutes to pass, repeat the procedure exactly, recording in Table 18.1 the number of songs and the minimum approach distance. In order for the test to be fair, we have to eliminate the so-called order effect, any response difference to the two tape cassettes stemming from the simple fact that one had to precede the other in time. We will take care of this potential problem by playing the two tapes in reverse sequence. Allow another 30 minutes to pass before testing "stranger song" again, then finish with a 30-minute rest period followed by "neighbor song." Now do the entire experiment again, this time using the second neighbor as the test bird. Reverse the sequence of playbacks to balance the design: stranger, neighbor, neighbor, stranger. Record your results for Bird 2 in Table 18.1.

Calculate the average responses of each bird to songs of neighbor and stranger, and add them to Table 18.1. If the averages are quite different, you could conclude that Song Sparrows are capable of discriminating between familiar and unfamiliar songs. Do your results suggest whether a neighbor or stranger is a greater threat to a bird's territory? You can obtain a more precise evaluation of the hypotheses by following the statistical analysis presented below.

Other questions about the function of singing and song recognition are approachable using playbacks. For example, is recognition of neighbor song place-specific? What happens if a male hears a neighbor singing from the "wrong" side of his territory? Do males become less aggressive as the breeding season progresses through egg, nestling, and fledgling stages? How does a bird respond to his own song? Song Sparrows sing in the fall as well as in the spring. Are their aggressive responses to neighbors and strangers the same during both seasons? Do sedentary males respond to playbacks in the winter when they normally do not sing?

Statistical analysis.

The null hypothesis states that singing and approach are no different in response to neighbor and stranger song. One alternative hypothesis predicts a stronger response to the neighbor, while the other alternative predicts the stranger will evoke a more aggressive reaction. The Median Test explained in Appendix 1 can be used to decide whether any variation in response to the two playbacks could have been due simply to chance at the 5% level of confidence. For this project, quite a bit more work is needed before the analysis can be run. You now have information for two birds, and you probably should build this number to at least 12 or 14. When you have, arrange your values in Tables 18.2 and 18.3, then proceed according to the appendix.

Further reading.

Baker, M. C. 1983. Sharing of vocal signals among Song Sparrows. *Condor* **85**: 482-490.

Harris, M. A. and R. E. Lemon. 1974. Songs of Song Sparrows: reactions of males to songs of different localities. *Condor* 76:33-44.

Weeden, J. S. and J. B. Falls. 1959. Differential responses of male Ovenbirds to recorded songs of neighboring and more distant individuals. *Auk* **76**: 342-351.

Table 18.1. Response of Song Sparrows to songs of immediate neighbors and strangers of the same dialect

Bird number	Playback	Songs during 5 minutes	Minimum approach to recorder (m)	Playback	Songs during 5 minutes	Minimum approach to recorder (m)
1	Neighbor song (play-back 1)			Stranger song (play-back 2)		
	Neighbor song (play-back 4)			Stranger song (play-back 3)		
Averages:						
2	Neighbor song (play-back 2)			Stranger song (play-back 1)		
	Neighbor song (play-back 3)			Stranger song (play-back 4)		
Averages:						

Table 18.2. Observed and expected numbers of songs during 5 minutes in response to playbacks of neighbor and stranger songs

	Neighbor song playback	Stranger song playback	Row total
Number of birds singing more than or equal to the median number of songs	Observed / Expected	Observed / Expected	
Number of birds singing fewer than the median number of songs	Observed / Expected	Observed / Expected	
Column total			

Table 18.3. Observed and expected minimum approach distance during 5 minutes in response to playbacks of neighbor and stranger songs

	Neighbor song playback	Stranger song playback	Row total
Number of birds approaching greater or equal to the median distance	Observed ⟋ Expected	Observed ⟋ Expected	
Number of birds approaching less than the median distance	Observed ⟋ Expected	Observed ⟋ Expected	
Column total			

19

If You Help a Robin Feed His Nestlings, Does He Defend a Bigger Territory?

COST-BENEFIT ANALYSIS, originally developed and applied to human economics, is becoming extremely useful in understanding bird economics. From this viewpoint, natural selection has favored the survival and reproduction of birds whose behavior returns the greatest benefit per unit cost. Cost-benefit analysts have tried to predict where birds should look for food, what kinds of food they should eat (which we explored in Chapter 11), how many eggs they should lay, and other life-history activities. In this project, we will test a new cost-benefit hypothesis concerning territory size.

Consider an American Robin setting up his breeding territory in your backyard or in the park down the street. Can we construct any sensible hypothesis concerning how big his territory should be? Let's consider separately what happens to benefits and costs as the area he defends gets larger. We know that robins feed their young with food caught in their territory. Thus, there must be some absolutely minimum territory size, because a robin defending a smaller area would not have access to enough food to raise even one nestling. Conversely, robins can only incubate so many eggs at once and, regardless of food supply, they can only transport some maximum amount of food per day to their offspring. This means that it does a robin no good to defend a very large territory if something else such as incubation ability or food delivery rate limits the number of young it can raise. On the benefit side, then, we can imagine a minimum and a maximum territory size for a male robin. Between these two extremes, the more area he defends, the more young he can produce, and the greater his evolutionary success.

What about the cost associated with being territorial? Energy and time spent in defense are the cost of being territorial and, all else being equal, these must increase as the territory gets larger. According to the cost-benefit perspective, a robin should pick a territory size that gives him the largest difference between benefit and cost, that is, the largest benefit-cost ratio. Therefore, the ingredients of territory size are the density of the food supply, which determines the benefits, and the density of intruders, which determines the time and energy costs of defense.

General hypotheses like this one are of little value unless they can be tested, so we will derive and test one prediction. Territories of many species are known to become smaller as the breeding season advances. Male songbirds defend a large area during mate-attraction, courtship, and incubation, but the territory shrinks dramatically during the nestling and fledgling stages. Cost-benefit theory would maintain that territory size shrinks because of increased costs. During early spring and through incubation, the male has few duties besides territorial defense. However, once nestlings hatch, natural selection would favor fathers that spend a great deal of time and energy catching food for their offspring. Males that spend too much time defending territories would raise fewer young. Once the nestlings hatch, males should spend less time in defense, and this means that territory size should become smaller. What would happen if we made it possible for a robin to feed his nestlings very easily and quickly? The cost-benefit hypothesis would predict that his territory size should not shrink; it should remain as large as during courtship and incubation time. It is this prediction we will test.

The first thing we need is a large supply of nestling-robin food, namely worms. Early in the spring, gather several hundred worms and store them in coffee cans in a refrigerator. Use a 50:50 ratio of worm volume and soil volume in each can. The easiest way to accumulate worms is to catch nightcrawlers on the surface of lawns during rainy nights.

To begin testing the prediction, select a male robin defending his territory in early spring. Males are slightly larger than females and have slightly brighter orange breasts. Heads of males are coal black, while females have charcoal-gray caps. As you did with Song Sparrows in Chapter 18, determine the robin's territorial boundaries by filling in a detailed map of the area with points corresponding to song perches and boundary disputes. Be careful never to mistake your bird for one of his neighbors.

Next, you must find the nest in your bird's territory. Early-spring nests are often placed in conifers if these are available, otherwise they are to be found in forks of deciduous trees, often next to the main trunk. As you may have noticed, robins build an outer layer of coarse grass and mud, line it with a cup of fine grass, and lay eggs of "robin's egg blue." Each day after you have found the nest, check its contents just before dusk when the female has left briefly to feed, drink, and bathe. Also, add more points to your map of the male's territory each day.

On the day that the nestlings hatch, start making your worm supply available. Line the bottom of a deep-sided container such as a dishpan with a 2.5-cm thick layer of paper towels and soak them with water. Next, cut up a brown kraft-paper shopping bag and lay it over the soaked towels so its edges extend up the sides of the container; this will prevent the worms from crawling under the towels. Place the container on the grass about 8 m from the nest. The best location for the worm box might be under a tree in which your robins often perch, so they can see into it and so the tree's shade will help keep the worms from drying out. Each morning for the next two or three days, add enough water to soak the kraft paper and paper towels and sprinkle in several dozen worms. When the nestlings are still small, it might be a good practice to provide small worms, or to cut large nightcrawlers into several pieces. After the robins are carrying worms from your container to their nestlings, you are ready to start the test. Let's say that from your daily nest check you know the nestlings are now four days old, and we know that baby robins leave the nest at about 14 days of age. We, therefore, have 10 days for the experiment, which we will call day 1 through day 10. Early on day 1, stock the container. That afternoon when you come home from school or work, or all day if possible, use a new map to pinpoint the male robin's singing locations. Also, use a stopwatch to record the total number of minutes he spends singing during one particular sample hour, say 18:00-19:00 (6 to 7 p.m.). Here, we do not want the total number of minutes of actual sound production, but rather the number of minutes sitting on song perches while singing; in short, the total length of "song bouts" during the hour. Early the next morning (day 2), carefully remove all the worms from the container so it will be empty throughout the day. The male will have to work hard throughout day 2 finding food for his nestlings. That afternoon, record his song perch locations on a new map, and record total length of song bouts from 18:00 to 19:00. Continue this procedure until the young leave the nest: worms on days 3, 5, 7, and 9, and no worms on days 4, 6, 8, and 10. Each day, make a new map of song perches used, and do a separate count of song bout minutes during the hour from 18:00 to 19:00.

After the little ones have gone from the nest, take each map and draw straight lines between adjacent outermost song perches used. We will operationally consider territory size to be the area bounded by the straight lines. Measure off the distance between two of these outermost song perches, and use this distance to draw a grid pattern over your map, as detailed in Figure 19.1. Total the whole and fractional grid squares to determine the area

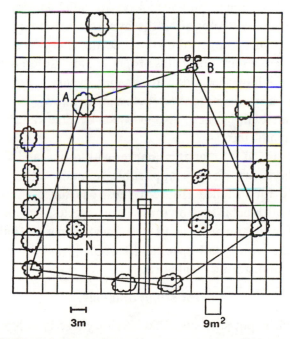

Fig. 19.1. Method of determining territory size. The distance between **A** and **B** was measured as 24 m. The rest of the territory, including the house, garage, driveway, and trees, was marked off in a 3-m grid, the width of each grid square corresponding to one-eighth the map distance between **A** and **B**. The territory size, determined by adding whole and partial grid squares, was 1,652 m². **N** marks the nest site.

of territory defended on each day, and enter these results in Table 19.1. Place your total song bout lengths for each day in Table 19.2. Calculate average territory size and average song bout length for "worm days" and for "no-worm days" and add these to the bottom of the appropriate table.

The hypothesis stated that territory size would shrink once a male was required to devote time and energy to feeding nestlings. We predicted that a superabundant source of food nearby would lessen considerably the time and energy needed to feed young, and would permit a male to maintain a large territory. Compare your average results for worm days and no-worm days. If territory size and song bout length on worm days are much larger, you might conclude you have supported the hypothesis that territory size is at least partially controlled by the time and energy costs involved. If your averages are fairly close together, any difference between them could have been due to chance events. Performing the statistical analysis described below will allow you to decide whether a real difference exists between average values at the 5% level of significance.

I have carried through this chapter with robins and worms, but the methods are directly applicable to many other territorial songbirds, for instance House Wrens, chickadees, titmice, nuthatches and bluebirds. For these latter species, substitute mealworms for earthworms. Cut the mealworms in half if you experiment with small species. (See Chapter 11 for notes on obtaining and storing mealworms.)

Statistical analysis.

The null hypothesis says that territory size is independent of defense costs. The alternative hypothesis maintains that defense costs at least partially determine territory size, and predicts that an artificially-produced increase in energy and time left over from feeding nestlings will be used to hold a territory larger than otherwise possible. Testing this prediction statistically requires a good deal more effort because we need records from 12 to 15 breeding attempts. As you accumulate average values for song bout length and territory size, enter them in Table 19.3. When you have records for 12 to 15 breeding attempts, arrange your values in Tables 19.4 and 19.5, then proceed with Median Tests as outlined in Appendix 1.

If your χ^2 values for song bout length and territory size are greater than those in Table A1.2 with one degree of freedom, you can reject the null hypothesis and conclude that defense costs at least partially determine territory size.

Further reading.

There are not yet any articles in North American ornithological journals concerning cost-benefit analyses of territory size. The references below are available in the biological science libraries of many colleges and universities.

Davies, N.B. 1978. Ecological questions about territorial behaviour. In: *Behavioural ecology: an evolutionary approach.* J.R. Krebs and N.B. Davies, eds. Oxford, Blackwell Scientific Publications.

MacLean, S.F., Jr. and T.R. Seastedt. 1979. Avian territoriality: sufficient resources or interference competition. *American Naturalist* **114**:308-312.

Myers, J.P., P.G. Connors, and F.A. Pitelka. 1981. Optimal territory size and the Sanderling: compromises in a variable environment. In: *Foraging behavior: ecological, ethological and psychological approaches.* A.C. Kamil and T.D. Sargent, eds. New York, Garland STPM Press.

Table 19.1. Territory sizes of a male robin on days when he was, or was not, provided with worms to feed his nestlings

Day number	"Worm territory" size (m^2)	Day number	"No-worm territory" size (m^2)
1			
		2	
3			
		4	
5			
		6	
7			
		8	
9			
		10	
Average = _____		Average = _____	

Table 19.2. Total time of song bouts during one hour of a male robin on days when he was, or was not, provided with worms to feed his nestlings

Day number	"Worm song bout" length (minutes)	Day number	"No-worm song bout" length (minutes)
1			
		2	
3			
		4	
5			
		6	
7			
		8	
9			
		10	
Average = _____		Average = _____	

Table 19.3. Average territory sizes and song-bout lengths of male robins on days when they were, or were not, provided with worms to feed their nestlings

Robin number	Average "worm" territory size (m²)	Average "no-worm" territory size (m²)	Average "worm" song-bout length (minutes)	Average "no-worm" song-bout length (minutes)
1				
2				
3				
4				
5				
6				
7				
8				
9				
10				
11				
12				
13				
14				
15				

Table 19.4. Observed and expected territory sizes of "worm" and "no-worm" male robins

	"Worm" territories	"No-worm" territories	Row total
Number of average territory sizes larger than or equal to the common median territory size	Observed _____ Expected	Observed _____ Expected	
Number of average territory sizes smaller than the common median territory size	Observed _____ Expected	Observed _____ Expected	
Column total			

Table 19.5. Observed and expected song-bout lengths of "worm" and "no-worm" male robins

	"Worm" song-bouts	"No-worm" song-bouts	Row total
Number of average song-bout lengths greater than or equal to the common median song-bout length	Observed ⟋ Expected	Observed ⟋ Expected	
Number of average song-bout lengths less than the common median song-bout length	Observed ⟋ Expected	Observed ⟋ Expected	
Column total			

20

Do City Lights Attract or Repel Nocturnal Migrants?

A S I write on a lovely late-April evening, warm air is moving
northward on the back side of a high pressure system, and
high overhead a delicate veil of songbirds is wafting by. These
migrants took wing shortly after sunset and will ride the tailwind
for six or eight hours, and for several hundred miles. Tomorrow, I
may welcome home the first Northern Oriole, Scarlet Tanager
and Rose-breasted Grosbeak.

During the last several decades, we have learned astounding
things about bird migration and navigation. Nocturnal migrants
can chart their course by the stars and by the earth's magnetic
field. The program telling them how far to migrate appears to be
at least partially inborn. Songbirds fly non-stop across the Gulf of
Mexico, and from New
England to the Bahamas
and on into the Caribbean.
Remarkable ingenuity
and technology have
fostered these find-
ings. Radar studies
have followed indi-
vidual migrants. Birds
have been fitted with
bar magnets or frosted

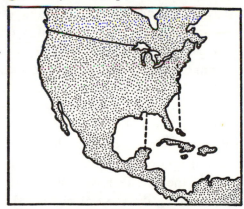

contact lenses. Migrants have been dropped from weather balloons
and asked to fly off wearing radio-transmitters. Experiments have
been performed in planetariums, pressure chambers and rooms
surrounded by magnetic coils. It has been an exciting area of
ornithology.

141

One aspect of bird migration needs further attention. How are the artifacts of man affecting avian navigation? Migrating birds see the stars and sense magnetic fields. We strew their flight paths with glowing cities, radio towers, and power generators. Are we jamming their sensory receptors and hindering their movements? This project checks to see whether migrating birds are thrown off course by urban concentrations of lights. S. A. Gauthereaux, Jr. of Clemson University has developed a method for counting migrants flying through the beam of a vertically-directed spotlight. We will use his technique to evaluate the hypothesis that city lights deflect nocturnal migrants from their normal flight path. You will need a 12-volt spotlight, a wooden box, wire leads, and binoculars or, preferably, a telescope.

Make the box with a square opening at the top. Opposite sides should be slightly closer together than the diameter of the spotlight. When the box sits on the ground, the spotlight should rest on all four sides and should point straight up. Use an extension cord to connect the spotlight to your car battery. You may wish to add an on-off switch between spotlight and battery. As an additional refinement, if alternating current is available, you can attach a 12 volt-110 volt transformer to the box and wire it into the circuit between spotlight and house current.

Our hypothesis states that city lights either repel or attract migrants. We derive the prediction that if we sample two locations along a line approximately perpendicular to wind direction, different numbers of birds should fly through the spotlight beam shining up from a lighted city than from the darker areas to either side of the city. Pick an east-west road crossing a city near you. Drive along the road at night and find a spotlighting location within the city, such as a park or shopping center parking lot, or you may find that your own backyard is a perfectly adequate location. Now find the second location by driving out of the city along the same road until the surrounding light intensity becomes noticeably reduced. The closest "exurbia" or farmland should suffice. As we will see in a minute, there is a reason why the two points should be no farther apart than necessary. Make arrangements for night work at both sites with landowners, sheriffs, police, etc.

Now we need favorable weather. Weather patterns over most of North America consist of alternating high and low pressure cells moving from west to east. Winds move clockwise around high pressure centers and they move counterclockwise around low pressure centers. We want to study spring migration in southerly winds and fall migration in northerly air, for these are the conditions when most birds migrate in the spring and fall, respectively. Carefully monitor television or newspaper weather maps. In the spring, look for conditions where a high pressure system is just east of you and a low pressure cell is just to the west. The winds in between will be from the south. In the fall, wait for a low to the east and a high to the west. Winds in between will be from the north. One other matter needs scrutiny. Previous studies have found that response to lights by migrating birds differs under clear and cloudy skies. Reduce the likelihood of ambiguous results by waiting for conditions where clouds obscure 50% or less of the night sky. On a night when the correct weather is predicted, flip a coin, heads for the city and tails for the country. Drive to the location dictated by the coin toss and set up your equipment by the time darkness falls. Place the box on the ground and align the spotlight vertically. Hook up the wires and turn on the light. Lie on your back and direct your telescope or binoculars up the axis of the spotlight. If you are using a telescope, a small tripod will give steadier viewing and reduce arm fatigue. Set some arbitrary starting time, such as 21:00 (9:00 p.m.), and count the number of birds you see flying through the beam of the spotlight during the next 15 minutes. Record the total in Table 20.1. Then gather up all your gear, jump into your car, bus, or subway, and head for the other site. Set things up there as quickly as possible, and, again, record in Table 20.1 the number of migrants flying through the beam in 15 minutes. Now flip a coin. Depending on the outcome, your next pair of records will be either city-country or country-city. Continue taking pairs of 15-minute samples until you wish to stop or until the migration wave thins perceptibly. Incidentally, if a car battery powers your light, you may want to recharge it occasionally by running the car's engine.

After you have 15 or 20 pairs of counts, you are ready to evaluate the hypothesis. Calculate average sightings per 15 minutes at the two locations and enter them at the bottom of Table 20.1. If the average values are very different, you might conclude that the bright lights, or perhaps some other factor associated with cities, have a strong influence on the flight path of nocturnally-migrating birds. If your average numbers are fairly close together, you might follow the statistical procedures at the end of this chapter to find out whether chance events could have accounted for the difference.

I have constructed this project so it can be done by one person, as can all the projects in this book. In this particular case, however, having more than one experimenter would be very useful, because then city and country spotlighting could be done simultaneously. Records would come in more quickly since you could eliminate travel time between the two sites. Simultaneous counting also has the advantage of guaranteeing nearly identical prevailing weather at the two sites. If you have two or a small group of workers available, divide into two parties and agree on the precise time periods for record-keeping before beginning each night's work.

The spotlight method can be used to study a number of questions about nocturnal migration. For example, is activity greater on clear than on cloudy or foggy nights? Do cities disrupt migration paths under heavy cloud? Do songbirds follow river valleys or mountain ridgelines at night? Do they skirt around large lakes? How closely correlated are migrant numbers and tail winds?

Statistical analysis.

The null hypothes states that cities have no effect on the flight paths of nocturnal migrants. The alternative hypothesis claims that cities either deflect or attract migrants, and predicts different numbers of birds passing over a lighted city and over nearby darker country locations. The Median Test, outlined in Appendix 1, can provide a basis for deciding whether to reject the null or alternative hypothesis at the 5% level of confidence. Find the common median of both sets of records, arrange your results in Table 20.2, and go on to calculate the χ^2 value.

Further reading.

Avery, M., P.F. Springer and J.F. Cassel. 1976. The effects of a tall tower on nocturnal bird migration—a portable ceilometer study. *Auk* **93**:281-291.

Gauthreaux, S.A., Jr. 1969. A portable ceilometer technique for studying low-level nocturnal migration. *Bird-Banding* **40**:309-320.

Gauthreaux, S.A., Jr. 1971. A radar and direct-visual study of passerine spring migration in southern Louisiana. *Auk* **88**:343-365.

Table 20.1. Numbers of nocturnal migrants passing through a spotlight beam during 15-minute periods at city and country locations

Pair of records	Date	Time of 15-minute period (e.g. 23:15-23:30)	Number of birds over city	Number of birds over country
1 1				
2 2				
3 3				
4 4				
5 5				
6 6				
7 7				
8 8				
9 9				
10 10				

Table 20.1. Numbers of nocturnal migrants passing through a spotlight beam during 15-minute periods at city and country locations (continued)

Pair of records	Date	Time of 15-minute period (e.g. 23:15-23:30)	Number of birds over city	Number of birds over country
11				
11				
12				
12				
13				
13				
14				
14				
15				
15				
16				
16				
17				
17				
18				
18				
19				
19				
20				
20				

Average = _____   Average = _____

Table 20.2. Observed and expected numbers of migrants per 15-minutes at city and country locations

	City location	Country location	Row total
Number of records greater than or equal to the common median	Observed / Expected	Observed / Expected	
Number of records less than the common median	Observed / Expected	Observed / Expected	
Column total			

21

Does Woodlot Size Determine Species Abundance in Winter?

ONE of the central questions in ecology asks why are there so many species of animals. Over the last decade or two, workers have used islands, in oceans and lakes, and land-locked *habitat islands*, to search for answers. A general conclusion has been that species numbers increase with the area of the island, whether it be a spruce-covered outlyer in the Gulf of Maine or an oak-hickory woodlot in a sea of Ohio corn fields. As one example, A.E. Galli, C.F. Leck, and their colleagues at Rutgers University have studied the relationship between the size of an isolated woodland and the number of bird species breeding there. In agreement with results from studies of other

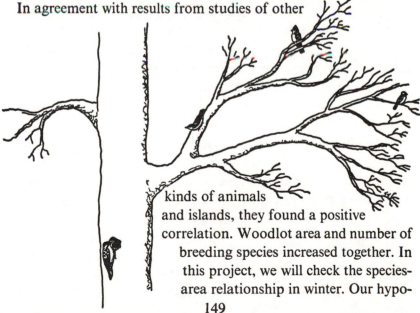

kinds of animals and islands, they found a positive correlation. Woodlot area and number of breeding species increased together. In this project, we will check the species-area relationship in winter. Our hypo-

149

thesis holds that the number of bird species wintering in a woodlot is a positive function of the woodlot's area.

The United States Geological Survey has produced topographical maps of the entire country. These may be examined in the offices of state geology and natural resources departments, at county seats, and in university and municipal libraries. The green areas on the maps denote wooded habitat. On maps of your area, locate 15 or 20 woodlands ranging in size from less than 1 to 20 or 25 hectares, and sharing the following characteristics: (1) relatively flat topography, (2) absence of large streams or rivers, and (3) isolation from other woodlands by pastures or tilled fields. Using the scale shown on the map, calculate the area of each woodlot to the nearest half hectare. Here in the midwest, most of our woodlands have nice straight boundaries. Estimation of area will be more complicated in hillier country where woodlands are irregular in form.

Drive out and inspect each of your selections to make sure it hasn't been destroyed or heavily timbered recently. While gaining permission from each owner to perform your project on his property, arrange to census each area three times over the course of the winter. Although I have never checked in any organized fashion, it is my impression that wintering birds are least disturbed if the field worker wears brown, tan and/or gray clothing. If you decide to stay with such dull-colored attire, **avoid all field work during deer-hunting season!**

Although many techniques exist for censusing birds, none is completely satisfactory. We will use a total-count belt-transect method, for which you will need a compass and notebook. Start at the southwest corner of a woodland and, guided by your compass, pace off 25 m due east as shown in Figure 21.1. Now turn to the left and walk into and all the way through the woods following your compass due north. As you walk slowly and quietly along this line, stop every 50 m or so and record in your notebook the species identity of each bird seen or heard within a

25-m strip on either side of the line. When you come to the north edge of the woods, turn right and walk due east for 50 m. Then turn right and follow your compass due south through the woodland, recording as before the species of birds within 25 m of the line. Continue this pattern of north and south transits until you have monitored the entire woodlot. We know that cold, windy weather reduces the detectability of birds in winter, so confine your censusing to reasonably calm, warm conditions. At the close of each census, transfer records from your field notebook to Table 21.1. When you have accomplished three surveys of each wooded area, calculate average species numbers and add them to the table.

Our hypothesis predicts that woodlot area and species number increase together. Mark Figure 21.2 with points corresponding to each pair of numbers from Table 21.1. If all your points lie close to an imaginary line from lower left to upper right, you may conclude you have supported the hypothesis. Suppose your result is not so clear as this. Maybe there is a suggestion of a trend from lower left to upper right in your graph, but some scatter is all too evident. Might your apparent correlation be due to some chance event during censusing? The statistical analysis at the end of this chapter can furnish a clear basis for evaluating the hypothesis.

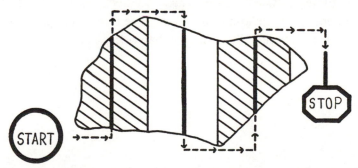

Fig. 21.1. The technique for censusing bird species in a woodland. The heavy lines show four north-south transects located 50 m apart. Cross-hatched or open areas represent 25-m strips on either side of a census line in which species are recorded. Dashed lines are paced off while establishing the positions of census transects.

Your results can be used to explore other questions. For example, do species-area curves diverge for seed-eaters, insect-eaters, and omnivores? Is there a body size-area correlation? Study of habitat islands is needed to underpin conservation work. Suppose you are concerned with an apparent down-turn in the number of Pileated Woodpeckers in your area, an all too common occurrence as woodstoves proliferate. What is the minimum area of woodland required by this species in your part of the country? In general, how great an expanse of woods is necessary before truly forest species such as nuthatches and woodpeckers join "edge" species like Common Cardinals and Rufous-sided Towhees? Suppose the Nature Conservancy of your state wishes to purchase a woodland large enough to contain all breeding and wintering species in your region. How large must it be? How great an area of native or reclaimed prairie do Upland Sandpipers require? What is the species-area curve for marsh islands in farmland? If we are going to preserve habitat islands from ploughs and cement mixers, we need some rational basis for deciding how large they must be. Suppose you know that 40 hectares of some particular habitat type is large enough to house all native bird species that use that habitat in your region, and you raise funds sufficient to purchase 80 hectares of that habitat. Prudence might dictate that you acquire two tracts of equal area rather than just one that is larger than necessary.

Statistical analysis.

The null hypothesis says that species number and woodlot size are unrelated. The alternative hypothesis predicts a positive correlation between the two quantities. The Spearman Rank Correlation analysis can be used in deciding whether to reject the null or alternative hypothesis at the 5% level. Arrange your results in Table 21.2 and follow directions in Appendix 2.

Further reading.

Galli, A.E., C.F. Leck, and R.T.T. Forman. 1976. Avian distribution patterns in forest islands of different size in central New Jersey. *Auk* **93**:356-364.
MacArthur, R.H. 1964. Environmental factors affecting bird species diversity. *Ecology* **42**:594-598.

Table 21.1. Numbers of wintering bird species censused in woodlots of different sizes

| Woodlot number | Woodlot area (hectares) | Number of bird species | | | Average number of bird species |
		1st census	2nd census	3rd census	
1					
2					
3					
4					
5					
6					
7					
8					
9					
10					
11					
12					
13					
14					
15					
16					
18					
19					
20					

Table 21.2. Numbers necessary to analyze the correlation between woodlot area and number of wintering bird species

Woodlot number	Area (hectares)	Average number of bird species	Rank of area	Rank of number of bird species	Difference between ranks	Difference between ranks squared
1						
2						
3						
4						
5						
6						
7						
8						
9						
10						
11						
12						
13						
14						
15						
16						
17						
18						
19						
20						

$$\sum \text{Diff.} = 0 \qquad \sum \text{Diff}^2 = \underline{\hspace{2cm}}$$

22

Do Populations of Black-capped and Carolina Chickadees Ebb and Flow?

ONE of the great assets of the amateur ornithologist is time. The professional must produce a continuous stream of finished projects in order to move up the job ladder, or obtain tenure. Twenty-five- to 30-year enterprises are not commonly undertaken by professionals. The long-term study is almost the exclusive province of the amateur. This project falls into the long-term category.

In my part of the country, Carolina Chickadees are permanent residents. Black-capped Chicadees sometimes join us for the winter, then retreat north-ward as little as a few dozen kilometers to breed. In the summer, the ranges of these two species do not overlap; they abut or remain narrowly separated along an east-west line from New Jersey to the Great Plains. By performing the project outlined here over a number of years, you may be able to discover what factor sets the breeding season boundary between the southern border of the Black-capped Chickadee and

156

the northern extreme of the Carolina. As the Black-capped is northern and the Carolina is southern, one hypothesis might be advanced that the boundary line is controlled by winter temperature. Hard, cold winters favor survival of the Black-capped Chickadee, so the boundary moves south; mild, easy winters favor the Carolina, so the boundary moves north. This hypothesis leads to the prediction that average daily temperature and the latitude of the boundary between the two species during the following breeding season show a positive relationship, the warmer the winter, the farther north the boundary.

To test this prediction, pick a 200-kilometer segment of a highway that runs approximately north-south and crosses the boundary between the two chickadees' breeding ranges. If you are not sure where the boundary is, consult a veteran birder, your local Audubon Society or the Biology Department at the nearest college. On a road map, denote the south end of your highway route as the 0 point and then mark the map at 5-km intervals north to the 200-km limit. Remember, you will be doing the project over a number of years, so try to avoid roadways in the path of creeping shopping-centeritis.

Every spring when the chickadees at home tell you it is time, census your highway for singing males of the two species. Pull off at each 5-km interval, locate the nearest appropriate habitat, and listen for songs. As you know, the two-note song of the Black-capped can be distinguished from the four-note song of the Carolina. Using BCC and CC as codes, record in Table 22.1 the species you hear singing at each 5-km interval. It is conceivable that at a boundary point you might hear both species singing. Repeat this procedure over a number of years.

Our hypothesis states that the colder the preceding winter's average daily temperature, the farther south you will hear Black-capped Chickadees singing during the following spring. Find the average daily temperature for the three months of December through February during the previous winter. You can either keep temperature records yourself or ask for them from the weather service at the nearest large airport. Enter each year's southernmost record of Black-capped Chickadee song and the average daily temperature of the previous winter in Figure 22.1. If the points in Figure 22.1 are arranged along a line from lower left to upper right, your results support the hypothesis that the boundary between breeding Carolina and Black-capped Chickadees is a function of the previous winter's temperature. If your results are less clear-cut and some scattering of points occurs, you might wish to pursue the statistical analysis at the end of this chapter to see whether a chance outcome could have been responsible.

The results from your first year's activity can be used to increase the precision of your study. Mark off your road map at 1-km intervals for 10 km on either side of the first year's boundary, and census each of these points in subsequent years.

We have been concerned here with the boundary between a species pair, but the censusing procedure can be used to study changes in the northern, southern, eastern, or western borders of single species in winter or summer. Other environmental factors besides temperature can also be examined. For instance, is the northern border of breeding Northern Bobwhites a function of the previous winter's snow depth in your area? Does the boundary line between Eastern and Western Meadowlarks change with average annual rainfall? Is the northern boundary of wintering Rufous-sided Towhees a function of average winter temperature? Answers to these and similar questions require long-term study, the special province of the amateur.

Statistical analysis.

The null hypothesis says there is no relationship between winter temperature and the boundary between breeding Black-capped and Carolina Chickadees. The alternative hypothesis maintains that the latitude of the boundary line is a positive function of average winter temperature, the warmer the previous winter, the farther north the boundary. These hypotheses can be evaluated with the Spearman Rank Correlation Test described in Appendix 2. Arrange your results in Table 22.2, then proceed to calculate Spearman's r. The fewer the tied ranks, the more powerful is the Spearman Test. I suggest you follow my earlier suggestion to mark off 1-km intervals for 10 km on either side of the first-year boundary. This procedure will increase the number of possible boundary points and, therefore, reduce the possibility of tied ranks.

Further reading.

Brewer, R. 1963. Ecological and reproductive relationships of Black-capped and Carolina Chickadees. *Auk* 80:9-47.

Merritt, P.G. 1981. Narrowly disjunct allopatry between Black-capped and Carolina Chickadees in northern Indiana. *Wilson Bulletin* 93:54-66.

Wiens, J.A. 1984. The place of long-term studies in ornithology. *Auk* 101: 202-203.

Table 22.1. Yearly presence of breeding Carolina and Black-capped Chickadees along a road transect crossing the boundary between the two species

Census location (km) from southern end of highway segment	Year and presence of singing Carolina (CC) and/or Black-capped (BCC) Chickadees							
	19 ___	19 ___	19 ___	19 ___	19 ___	19 ___	19 ___	19 ___
0								
5								
10								
15								
20								
25								
30								
35								
40								
45								
50								
55								
60								
65								
70								
75								
80								
85								
90								

Census location (km) from southern end of highway segment	Year and presence of singing Carolina (CC) and/or Black-capped (BCC) Chickadees							
	19 ___	19 ___	19 ___	19 ___	19 ___	19 ___	19 ___	19 ___
95								
100								
105								
110								
115								
120								
125								
130								
135								
140								
145								
150								
155								
160								
165								
170								
175								
180								
185								
190								
195								
200								

Table 22.2. Numbers needed to analyze the correlation between the southern boundary of breeding Black-capped Chickadees and the average daily temperature of the previous winter

Year	Southern-most census point	Average winter tempera-ture	Rank of southern-most census point	Rank of average winter tempera-ture	Difference between ranks	Difference between ranks squared
19 __						
19 __						
19 __						
19 __						
19 __						
19 __						
19 __						
19 __						
19 __						
19 __						
19 __						
19 __						
19__						
19 __						
19 __						

$\sum$Diff. = 0 $\sum$Diff.^{2} = _____

23

What To Do When You Know This Book.

L ET'S SUPPOSE you are now familiar with this book. You
have tried several projects and have worked out two or three
statistical analyses. Application of the scientific method to field
ornithology is no longer a mystery. In addition to your interest in
the kinds and numbers of birds,
you may now be asking
yourself new
kinds of
questions,
such as
why does
an Acorn
Woodpecker
help its
parents raise
its younger
siblings instead
of producing
offspring of its
own. Why might a female Red-
winged Blackbird share a male with
another female rather than find a mate for
herself? How much food per trip should a Mountain Bluebird
carry to its nestlings?

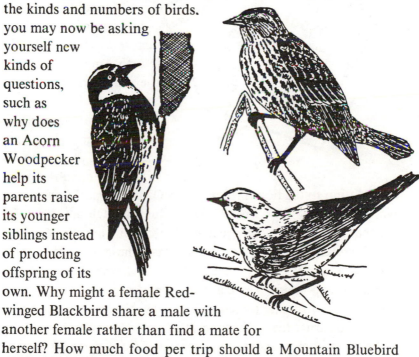

Where do questions like these come from? Sometimes, they are
inspired by bits of knowledge gathered from the actual watching
of birds. As you survey a flock of wintering gulls or chance upon a

163

breeding colony of Bank Swallows, try to assume a how-why frame of mind. Try to ask the questions about getting food, avoiding predators, and raising young that we have been dealing with in the preceding chapters.

The second major source of information leading to new questions is the published record. The *Auk, Condor, Wilson Bulletin,* and *Journal of Field Ornithology* are the four major journals of ornithological research published in North America. They are the sources of most of the articles in this book's Further reading sections. You might consider giving one or more of these journals a trial run. For subscription information to the first three, write to Ornithological Societies of North America, P.O. Box 21618, Columbus, Ohio 43221. The *Journal of Field Ornithology* may be ordered from the Membership Secretary, Box 797, Manomet, Massachusetts 02345.

Once a question is in hand, the search for answers often requires a hypothesis. There are no formal rules or procedures to follow in constructing these explanations. No one can teach you how to construct them. However, the recipe for every hypothesis in field ornithology contains ingredients from personal experience, the published record, or both. Hypotheses share the realm of creativity with poetry, symphonies, and sculpture. The great contributions to science have been new hypotheses, new creative answers to questions. Generating new explanations for what we find in nature, unlocking secrets, is the most exciting part of science.

Further reading.

Field ornithology deals primarily with the subdisciplines of biology called animal behavior and ecology, and their hybrids, behavioral ecology and sociobiology. The books listed below are not kid stuff, but all are written in clear, straightforward language. Taken together, they present an excellent summary of how field ornithology is one part of a larger enterprise concerning all groups of animals.

Alcock, J. 1984. *Animal behavior: an evolutionary approach.* Third edition. Sunderland, Mass., Sinauer.
Barash, D.P. 1977. *Sociobiology and behavior.* New York, Elsevier.
Colinvaux, P. 1973. *Introduction to ecology.* New York, Wiley.
Morse, D.H. 1980. *Behavioral mechanisms in ecology.* Cambridge, Mass., Harvard University Press.

Appendix I. The Chi-square Test and the Median Test

The foregoing projects have involved testing predictions we have derived from hypotheses. This appendix and the next one describe statistical tests that can help you decide whether the results you found matched our predictions or could have been due only to chance variation.

Using analytical statistics is not difficult. The best way to convince you of this is to take you through some examples. We will analyze statistically some possible results from studies of preferred tree height in Downy Woodpeckers (Chapter 2), preferred perch height in grassland birds (Chapter 3), and search paths of robins hunting worms (Chapter 6).

The Chi-square Test and the Median Test are the two procedures we will employ here and these are both called non-parametric tests. (Incidentally, Chi is pronounced as "ki.") This type of test does not depend on the assumption that results are part of a bell-shaped curve. The other class of statistical test is called parametric; tests of this second variety assume a bell-shaped curve. I will not deal any further with the theoretical underpinnings of analytical statistics for they are beyond the scope of this book. From now on we will be considering the practical use of Chi-square and Median Tests. There are many books describing the use of analytical statistics and two good ones are listed as Further reading at the close of this appendix.

The Chi-square Test of Goodness of Fit.

In the woodpecker project, you investigated which of three different heights of artificial trees the birds preferred for excavating. Results of this kind are called discontinuous or discrete because each record falls into one of several unique, separate categories. Sex, country of birth, and eye color are other kinds of discrete variables. The Chi-square Test may be used to analyze discrete results, so we will apply it to the choice of tree height by Downy Woodpeckers. What we want to know is did the choice of tree heights the birds made represent a real preference or could the results have been due solely to some chance, random variation in the birds' behavior. Our first step in deciding is to construct what is called a null hypothesis. Remember that the hypothesis we investigated in Chapter 2 said that Downy Woodpeckers have a preferred snag height in which to dig their cavities. The null hypothesis simply results from rewording our hypothesis in the negative. In this case, the null hypothesis states that Downy Woodpeckers *do not* have a preferred snag height for digging their cavities. Now that we have our null hypothesis, I want you to think of the original construction as the alternative hypothesis.

Null hypothesis: Downy Woodpeckers *do not* have a preferred snag height for digging their cavities.

Alternative hypothesis: Downy Woodpeckers *do* have a preferred snag height for digging their cavities.

Other null hypotheses might be, birds do not have different sexes, birds are not born in different countries, birds do not have different eye colors.

Our prediction about the woodpeckers was that if the alternative hypothesis is correct, the birds should have a definite preference among the three tree heights. Suppose we repeated the study 24 times and suppose eight birds chose 120-cm trees, eight birds chose 240-cm trees, and eight birds chose 360-cm trees. It certainly would appear that the woodpeckers had no particular preferred height and eight birds just happened to end up digging on each height tree. This could have occurred by chance alone. We would reject the alternative hypothesis that Downy Woodpeckers have a preferred tree height. Now consider a quite different result, no woodpeckers chose 120-cm trees or 240-cm trees and all 24 birds excavated in the 360-cm blanks. We would have to conclude that the species has a very definite preferred snag height and we would reject the null hypothesis that no preference exists. Unfortunately, results in field ornithology are almost never as clear-cut as these. As a more realistic case, let us suppose that of the 24 Downy Woodpeckers in our imaginary example, two chose the 120-cm trees, fifteen chose the 240-cm trees, and seven chose those 360-cm tall. We cannot be sure exactly what to conclude. Maybe this outcome could have been due to a definite preference for 240-cm trees along lines predicted by the alternative hypothesis, but maybe it was just due to chance variation commensurate with the null hypothesis, like throwing dice and turning up two sixes. We need some way of deciding the likelihood that this result was due to chance and not to any preference for a particular tree height. This is where the Chi-square Test can help. If the null hypothesis were correct and the birds had no preference for tree height, we would expect approximately equal use of all three tree heights. Given our sample size of 24, the *expected* number of cavities in each height would, therefore, be eight, but our imaginary project gave us *observed* results of two, fifteen, and seven cavities in the three tree heights. We want to know what is the probability that the observed and expected height selection differed due to chance variation alone and not due to a real preference for 240-cm trees. If we knew this probability, we could decide whether to reject the null or alternative hypothesis.

Scientists customarily use what is called the 5% level of rejection. If there is less than or equal to a 5% probability that observed and expected results differ solely due to random chance, they reject the null hypothesis. If the probability that the observed and expected values differ due to chance alone is greater than 5%, they reject the alternative hypothesis. To find this probability for our woodpecker choice, we start by constructing Table A1.1, which contains our observed results and those expected by the null hypothesis.

The Chi-square Test uses an elementary equation to find the value of a test statistic called χ^2. χ is the 22nd letter of the Greek alphabet and, like Chi, is pronounced as "ki." When referring to the test procedure we are discussing, we use the term, Chi-square, and when labelling the numerical value of the analytical statistic produced by this Chi-square test, we use χ^2. Let's calculate χ^2 for this example, then see how we use it to assess whether our observed results could have been due to chance. The equation for χ^2 is:

$$\chi^2 = \Sigma \; \frac{(\text{Observed - Expected})^2}{\text{Expected}}$$

In words, this equation says to take each expected value in Table A1.1 and subtract it from the corresponding observed value. Take the result and square it; that is, multiply it times itself. Then divide that result by the same original expected value. Since there are three pairs of observed and expected values in our example, we will perform this operation three times. Then add together the three resulting numbers (Σ means summation) to give us the value of χ^2. In our example:

$$\chi^2 = \frac{(2 - 8)^2}{8} + \frac{(15 - 8)^2}{8} + \frac{(7 - 8)^2}{8}$$

$$= \frac{(-6)^2}{8} + \frac{(7)^2}{8} + \frac{(-1)^2}{8}$$

$$= \frac{36}{8} + \frac{49}{8} + \frac{1}{8}$$

$$= 4.5 + 6.1 + 0.1$$

$$= 10.7$$

So $\chi^2 = 10.7$. The Chi-square Test procedure says that if this number is greater than the χ^2 value expected by chance at the 5% level, we reject the null hypothesis.

There is one more matter to be considered, something called degrees of freedom. Without going into the meaning of this quantity in any great detail, we will just note that degrees of freedom has to do with the number of expected values that may vary

Table A1.1. Expected and observed tree height preferences of Downy Woodpeckers

	Number of birds choosing 120-cm trees	Number of birds choosing 240-cm trees	Number of birds choosing 360-cm trees
Observed in our study	2	15	7
Expected due to chance alone	8	8	8

independently. Degrees of freedom are found by looking at a table of observed and expected values such as Table A1.1, which is called a contingency table. In Table A1.1, we have three columns of expected values with only one row in each column. In cases such as this where there is only one row, the degrees of freedom value is the number of columns minus one. We have three columns, so our degrees of freedom value is two.

Now we are ready to test our null and alternative hypotheses. Turn to the expected χ^2 values in Table A1.2. Here are listed the χ^2 values corresponding to a 5% probability that the difference between observed and expected results is due solely to chance. The χ^2 value corresponding to two degrees of freedom is 6.0. Our calculated χ^2 value of 10.7 is larger than 6.0, so we conclude there is less than a 5% chance that the preference of Downy Woodpeckers we observed was the result of random choice of tree height. We reject the null hypothesis and fail to reject the alternative hypothesis. This type of Chi-square Test is called a Chi-square Test of Goodness of Fit because it tests how good the fit is between observed values and those expected from random chance behavior. Our result only tells us that tree height selection was not random; it does not tell us how it was non-random. However, we can conclude that selection was non-random because Downy Woodpeckers showed a strong preference for 240-cm trees, a strong aversion to 120-cm trees, and no particular preference or aversion for 360-cm trees. As an exercise, you might calculate the χ^2 value for a case where seven birds chose 120-cm trees, 11 chose 240-cm trees and six chose 360-cm trees. Your χ^2 value should equal 1.7. Does this value suggest that the woodpeckers had a significant tree-height preference at the 5% level of rejection?

I need to tell you about one more general requirement for use of the Chi-square statistic. All expected values should be greater than five for the test to have validity. There are several rather involved ways to get around this requirement through manipulation of numbers, but they are beyond the scope of this book. The best way is simply to make sure you take large sample sizes. The larger the sample size, the greater is the likelihood that all expected values will be greater than five.

In summary, to perform the Chi-square Test of Goodness of Fit:

(1) Enter observed values (not percentages) in a contingency table. Such tables may be found at the ends of those chapters that suggest the use of the Chi-square Test.

(2) Calculate expected values by dividing the total number of observed values by the number of columns, or cells, in the table. All cells will have the same expected value.

(3) Use the equation to calculate χ^2.

(4) Compare your calculated χ^2 with the χ^2 value in Table A1.2 corresponding to your degrees of freedom. If the caculated χ^2 is greater than or equal to the tabulated χ^2, reject the null hypothesis at the 5% level of confidence. If the calculated χ^2 is less than the tabulated χ^2, reject the alternative hypothesis at the 5% level of confidence.

Table A1.2. χ^2 values at the 5% level of chance. If a calculated value of χ^2 is greater than or equal to the corresponding value in the table, we reject the null hypothesis and fail to reject the alternative hypothesis

Degrees of freedom	Value of χ^2
1	3.8
2	6.0
3	7.8
4	9.5
5	11.1
6	12.6
7	14.1
8	15.5
9	16.9
10	18.3

Chi-square Test of Heterogeneity.

Often we wish to know whether two or more sets of outcomes are more different than could be expected just due to chance. For example, do male and female Downy Woodpeckers prefer different snag heights for excavating? We can test whether the two sets of outcomes are different, or heterogeneous, by using what is called the Chi-square Test of Heterogeneity. The procedure is only slightly more involved than that just described for the Chi-square Test of Goodness of Fit.

Let's work through an example using some made-up results concerning perch height selection in grassland birds similar to those you might obtain by working through Chapter 3. Our imaginary hayfield has breeding Eastern Meadowlarks, Savannah Sparrows and Red-winged Blackbirds. We spend several days moving our quartet of perches around the field and recording landings of the three species on the four perch heights. Then we summarize our results in Table A1.3. Next, we add together the height values for each species and enter the row totals, 93, 78, and 86. We do the same thing for the three species' values at each perch height to obtain the column totals, 26, 73, 70, and 88. Add together the three row totals or the four column totals to find the grand total, 257 in our exercise. It is a useful check on your arithmetic to find the grand total both ways. If you do not get the same answer, you will need to find your error within the row or column totals.

Table A1.3. Some imaginary results of perch height choice by three grassland bird species

Species	Number of landings				
	30-cm perch	90-cm perch	150-cm perch	210-cm perch	Row total
Eastern Meadowlark	0	15	27	51	93
Red-winged Blackbird	9	6	31	32	78
Savannah Sparrow	17	52	12	5	86
Column total	26	73	70	88	257

Under the null hypothesis, we would expect no differences in the extent to which each perch height was used by the three species. To find our expected values, we have to work out the number of landings by each species on each perch height that would have occurred if all species used each height to the same extent. Let's find the expected number of Eastern Meadowlark landings on 30-cm perches. We know that meadowlarks accounted for 93 of the 257 total landings. If all species used each height to the same extent, we would expect the number of landings on 30-cm perches by meadowlarks to be proportional to the number of landings on all perches by meadowlarks. We will call the expected number of meadowlark landings on 30-cm perches X, and set up the proportion,

$$\frac{X}{26} = \frac{93}{257}$$

then solve for X:

$$257X = (26)(93)$$

$$X = \frac{(26)(93)}{257}$$

$$= 9.4$$

So, if all species had preferred each perch height to the same extent, as the null hypothesis states, we would expect 9.4 meadowlark landings on 30-cm perches. In general, to find any expected value, multiply its row total times its column total and divide by the grand total. I have worked out the expected values for our example and entered them, along with the observed values, in Table A1.4.

We have twelve pairs of observed and expected values. Just as we did in the Goodness-of-Fit Test, we calculate a χ^2 value using the

$$\chi^2 = \Sigma \frac{(\text{Observed} - \text{Expected})^2}{\text{Expected}}$$

equation, the only difference being the greater quantity of entries here. From Table A1.4, we assemble:

$$\chi^2 = \frac{(0 - 9.4)^2}{9.4} + \frac{(15 - 26.4)^2}{26.4} + \frac{(27 - 25.3)^2}{25.3} + \frac{(51 - 31.9)^2}{31.9}$$

$$+ \frac{(9 - 7.9)^2}{7.9} + \frac{(6 - 22.1)^2}{22.1} + \frac{(31 - 21.2)^2}{21.2} + \frac{(32 - 26.7)^2}{26.7}$$

$$+ \frac{(17 - 8.7)^2}{8.7} + \frac{(52 - 24.5)^2}{24.5} + \frac{(12 - 23.5)^2}{23.5} + \frac{(5 - 29.4)^2}{29.4}$$

$$= 9.4 + 4.9 + 0.1 + 11.4 + 0.2 + 11.7 + 4.5 + 1.0 + 7.9$$

$$+ 30.9 + 0.6 + 20.2$$

$$= 102.8$$

Table A1.4. Made-up observed and expected landings on different perch heights used in illustrating the Chi-square Test of Heterogeneity

Species	Landings on 30-cm perch		Landings on 90-cm perch		Landings on 150-cm perch		Landings on 210-cm perch		Row total
	Observed	Expected	Observed	Expected	Observed	Expected	Observed	Expected	
Eastern Meadowlark	0	9.4	15	26.4	27	25.3	51	31.9	93
Red-winged Blackbird	9	7.9	6	22.1	31	21.2	32	26.7	78
Savannah Sparrow	17	8.7	52	24.5	12	23.5	5	29.4	86
Column total	26		73		70		88		257

Calculators are very useful in dealing with bulky material like this, not only because they speed things up, but because they reduce the likelihood of an arithmetic error. As before, we now compare our calculated χ^2 with the appropriate value in Table A1.2. In Chi-square Tests of Heterogeneity, degrees of freedom equal to the number of rows minus one, times the number of columns minus one. We have three rows and four columns in our example, so degrees of freedom = (3 - 1) (4 - 1) = 2 × 3 = 6. At the 5% level of confidence, the tabulated χ^2 corresponding to six degrees of freedom is 12.6. Since our calculated χ^2 of 102.8 is larger, we reject the null hypothesis. Our test with Eastern Meadowlarks, Red-winged Blackbirds and Savannah Sparrows has supported the alternative hypothesis that species of grassland birds prefer different perch heights. From inspection of Tables A1.3 and A1.4, we conclude that the reason they differed was because in our imaginary study, meadowlarks showed a strong preference for the highest perch, blackbirds used mainly the two tallest locations, and the sparrow was very partial to the 90-cm height.

To summarize the steps in the Chi-square Test of Heterogeneity:
(1) Enter the observed values (not percentages) in a contingency table, and determine the row, column, and grand totals.
(2) Calculate the expected value for each cell by multiplying the row total times the column total and dividing by the grand total.
(3) Use the equation to calculate χ^2.
(4) Find degrees of freedom, which equal the number of rows minus one, times the number of columns minus one.
(5) Compare your calculated χ^2 with the χ^2 value in Table A1.2 corresponding to your degrees of freedom. If the calculated χ^2 is equal to or greater than the tabulated χ^2, reject the null hypothesis at the 5% level of confidence. If the calculated χ^2 is less than the tabulated χ^2, reject the alternative hypothesis at the 5% level of confidence.

Median Test.

In many projects, you will produce what are called continuous results. These are results that can be placed on a continuous scale such as weight, wing length, or flight velocity. Because the Chi-square Test may only be used with discrete data, we will use another technique, called the Median Test, to investigate hypotheses producing continuous data.

Let's examine some possible results from one project. Chapter 6 concerns the search paths of robins. One alternative hypothesis stated that after a stop producing a worm, a robin runs a shorter distance before stopping again than it does after a stop failing to produce a worm. The null hypothesis would have it that runs after successful and unsuccessful stops do not differ in average length. As length of run is a continuous variable, we will use the Median Test to decide between the null and alternative hypotheses. Say, we record the lengths of 15 runs after a robin catches a worm and 15 runs after unproductive stops, and we list them in Table A1.5.

The median of any group of numbers is the middle value. To perform the Median Test, we need to find the common median of both sets of run lengths combined. First, we list all 30 numbers in Table A1.5 from smallest to largest: 1, 1, 2, 2, 2, 3, 3, 4, 5, 6, 7, 7, 7, 8, 8, 9, 9, 10, 10, 11, 11, 12, 12, 12, 15, 15, 16, 16, 17, 20. Since we have 30 numbers, the middle value is halfway between rank 15 and rank 16. The 15th value is 8 and the 16th value is 9, so the value of the common median is 8.5 cm. Next, we find the number of runs for each group of robins longer than or equal to the common median, and the number of runs for each group of robins shorter than the common median. The common median is 8.5 cm, so we count up the number of runs for each group of robins longer than or equal to 8.5 cm, and the number shorter than 8.5 cm. These are shown as observed values in Table A1.6.

If the null hypothesis were correct, we would expect the proportion of all runs that consisted of runs longer than or equal to

Table A1.5. Possible run lengths of robins hunting worms

Record number	Run length after catching a worm (cm)	Run length after not catching a worm (cm)
1	7	10
2	10	12
3	15	17
4	2	16
5	3	7
6	5	9
7	9	8
8	1	2
9	12	11
10	4	16
11	7	9
12	2	20
13	6	15
14	1	12
15	3	11

the common median to be the same whether the robin had just caught a worm or not. The same would be true for runs shorter than the common median. We can calculate these expected values and then use the Chi-square procedure in deciding whether to reject the null or alternative hypothesis. If catching a worm has no effect on the length of the next run, then the number of runs longer than or equal to the common median for robins catching a worm should be proportional to the number of runs longer than or equal to the common median for both groups of robins combined. If we let X stand for the value expected in the upper left-hand box of Table

A1.6, then X should be in the same proportion to 15, the column total, as 16 is to 30, the grand total, or

$$\frac{X}{15} = \frac{16}{30}$$

Cross-multiplying gives us

$$30X = (15)(16)$$

$$X = \frac{(15)(16)}{30}$$

$$= 8$$

Table A1.6. Observed run lengths of robins relative to a common median run length of 8.5 cm

	Runs after worm	Runs not after worm	Row total
Number of runs longer than or equal to the common median	4	12	16
Number of runs shorter than the common median	11	3	14
Column total	15	15	30

So we expect eight of the 15 runs after a worm to be longer than or equal to the common median if the null hypothesis is correct. In general, the expected value for any cell is equal to its row total times its column total divided by the grand total. Doing this calculation for the other three expected values gives us the values shown in Table A1.7. In our example, the two categories of behavior, runs after worm and runs not after worm, had the same sample size of 15, but this procedure for determining expected values works even when the two sample sizes are unequal.

Table A1.7. Imaginary observed and expected run lengths of robins used to illustrate the Median Test

	Runs after worm	Runs not after worm	Row total
Number of runs longer than or equal to the common median	Observed 4 / 8 Expected	Observed 12 / 8 Expected	16
Number of runs shorter than the common median	Observed 11 / 7 Expected	Observed 3 / 7 Expected	14
Column total	15	15	30

Now we calculate the χ^2 value, again using the equation,

$$\chi^2 = \Sigma \frac{(\text{Observed - Expected})^2}{\text{Expected}}$$

$$\chi^2 = \frac{(4-8)^2}{8} + \frac{(12-8)^2}{8} + \frac{(11-7)^2}{7} + \frac{(3-7)^2}{7}$$

$$\chi^2 = \frac{(4)^2}{8} + \frac{(4)^2}{8} + \frac{(4)^2}{7} + \frac{(4)^2}{7}$$

$$\chi^2 = \frac{16}{8} + \frac{16}{8} + \frac{16}{7} + \frac{16}{7}$$

$$= 8.6$$

So the calculated χ^2 is 8.6. Our contingency table had two rows and two columns of expected values. Degrees of freedom are found by multiplying the number of rows minus one, times the number of columns minus one; $df=(r-1)(c-1)$. In this case, $df=(2-1)(2-1)=1$. We now enter Table A1.2. You recall that this table lists χ^2 values corresponding to a 5% probability that the difference between observed and expected results is due solely to chance. The χ^2 value corresponding to one degree of freedom is 3.8. Our calculated χ^2 value of 8.6 is greater than 3.8, so we conclude that the difference between lengths of run after catching a worm and not catching a worm could not have been due to chance alone. We reject the null hypothesis and accept the alternative hypothesis. Real robins will give you real numbers to test; the imaginary results here may have no relationship to what your robins actually do.

You may have noticed that the Median Test is just a way of converting a continuous variable such as run length into a discrete one such as number of runs shorter than the common median length. We then can do a Chi-square test on the discrete variable we have created. In this case, the Chi-square Test of Heterogeneity was appropriate.

In summary, to perform the Median Test:
(1) List together all the values in both groups from smallest to largest.
(2) Determine the value of the common median.
(3) For each group, count the number of values equal to or greater than the common median, and the number of values less than the common median. Enter these observed values in a 4-cell contingency table.
(4) Calculate the expected value for each cell by multiplying the row total times the column total and dividing by the grand total.
(5) Use the equation to calculate χ^2.
(6) Find degrees of freedom, which equal the number of rows minus 1, times the number of columns minus 1.
(7) Compare your calculated χ^2 with the χ^2 value in Table A1.2 corresponding to your degrees of freedom. If calculated χ^2 is equal to or greater than tabulated χ^2, reject the null hypothesis at the 5% level of confidence. If calculated χ^2 is less than tabulated χ^2, reject the alternative hypothesis at the 5% level of confidence.

Well, you have just been through some rather dense material. You might wish to go over this appendix again soon for it should become clearer as you become acquainted with the names for various quantities and manipulations. For Further reading, I have selected two books which explain statistics in straightforward language. Any good library will have a wider selection. I hope I have convinced you that statistical analyses can provide a strong base for deciding whether to support or reject any hypothesis, and are therefore the backbone of analytical ornithology.

Further reading.

Runyon, R.P. and A. Haber. 1971. *Fundamentals of behavioral statistics.* Addison-Wesley, Reading, Massachusetts.
Siegel, S. 1956. *Nonparametric statistics for the behavioral sciences.* McGraw-Hill, New York.

Appendix 2.
The Spearman Rank Correlation Test

The Chi-square Test and the Median Test described in Appendix 1 can tell us when one set of numbers differs from what we might expect by chance, or when two sets of numbers are more different from each other than expected by chance. Suppose, though, that we have a hypothesis which states that two kinds of quantities vary together in some predictable way. For example, the longer the wing length of any subspecies within a given species, the greater the distance it migrates, or the older the male Ruffed Grouse, the more females he mates with per breeding season. These are called positive correlations. The two quantities vary together such that as one gets larger, so does the other. Negative correlations can also be hypothesized where as one quantity gets larger, the other gets smaller. For example, as the average daily temperature during winter increases, the length of time that Northern Cardinals spend looking for food decreases, or the more turbid the water, the fewer fish Belted Kingfishers catch per hour.

We need some way of assessing whether the two quantities we measure actually are varying together as predicted by our hypothesis, or whether any apparent correlation produced is just due to the amount of variation in results we could expect from chance happenstance. Several analytical statistics are available which test the strength of a correlation. One of these, the Spearman Rank Correlation Test, will be used for this book's projects.

When applied to any two sets of results, the Spearman Test produces a Spearman Correlation Coefficient, r. This r can take values between -1 and +1. When $r = -1$, we have two sets of numbers that have a perfect negative correlation. That is, without exception, as the value of one quantity in our sample becomes larger, the value of the second quantity gets smaller. Similarly an $r = +1$ indicates a perfect positive correlation. Without exception, every larger value

185

of one quantity is accompanied by a larger value of the second quantity. If r varies between -1 and +1, what does $r = 0$ mean? It means that there is no correlation between the two quantities. They are completely independent of one another. If we tested the correlation between the number of songs per minute in Scarlet Tanagers and the number of bagel stands in the nearest city, we would probably calculate an r close to 0. In most cases, r will not equal -1, 0, or +1; it will be somewhere in the middle. Say we analyzed the correlation between the rate at which Cattle Egrets walked through a pasture looking for grasshoppers and the height of the grass, and we found that $t = -0.37$. We might suspect that the higher the grass, the slower the birds walked, but was the negative correlation strong enough, close enough to -1, to rule out the possibility that -0.37 was just due to chance? We want to know whether $r = -0.37$ is statistically different from $r = 0$. As part of the Spearman analysis we can compare calculated r with r in a table of values expected solely due to chance, just as we did with χ^2 values in Appendix 1.

Let's work through a Spearman Rank Correlation Test of some imaginary results from the fishing behavior of Great Blue Herons described in Chapter 7. Our hypothesis was that herons used average catch times to tell them what their giving-up time should be. We predicted that if our hypothesis were correct, then over a large range of habitats and seasons of the year, we should see a positive correlation between catch time and giving-up time. Now we can add that we predict r to be significantly greater than 0.

Let's assume that we do the study and determine the 15 pairs of average values shown in Table A2.1. You might want to construct a scattergram of these made-up results, as described in Chapter 7. The first step in the Spearman Analysis is to rank the values within each category from smallest to largest. Here, we assign ranks 1 through 15 to catch times, and do the same for giving-up times, as shown in the two left-hand columns of Table A2.2. Notice that some tied values occur in Table A2.1; there are two 30-second catch

Table A2.1. Some possible average catch times and giving-up times of Great Blue Herons fishing in 15 different habitats and/or on 15 different days

Habitat and/or day	Average catch time (in seconds)	Average giving-up time (in seconds)
1	122	107
2	66	32
3	79	61
4	94	111
5	43	48
6	64	72
7	30	34
8	91	76
9	110	119
10	76	90
11	61	90
12	104	59
13	67	64
14	30	46
15	92	90

times and three 90-second giving-up times. In these cases, we assign the mean rank to each of the tied scores, and the next higher score in the list receives the rank normally assigned to it. Thus, to values 30, 45, 60, 60, 60, and 90 seconds, we would give the ranks, 1, 2, 4, 4, 4, and 6.

The next step in the Spearman Test procedure is to find the difference between ranks for each pair of numbers and then square that difference, as shown in the two right-hand columns of Table A2.2. Find Σ Difference between ranks and Σ Difference² between ranks as shown at the bottom of Table A2.2. Although we will have no further use for Σ Difference, it is a good idea to calculate it anyway. Since Σ Difference must equal 0, it can give you a check on your arithmetic. If your Σ Difference does not sum to 0, you will want to go back and discover your error.

Table A2.2. Computational procedures for calculating Spearman's r

Habitat and/or day	Rank of average catch time	Rank of average giving-up time	Difference between ranks	Difference between ranks squared
1	15	13	2	4
2	6	1	5	25
3	9	6	3	9
4	12	14	-2	4
5	3	4	-1	1
6	5	8	-3	9
7	1.5	2	-0.5	0.25
8	10	9	1	1
9	14	15	-1	1
10	8	11	-3	9
11	4	11	-7	49
12	13	5	8	64
13	7	7	0	0
14	1.5	3	-1.5	2.25
15	11	11	0	0

$\sum$Diff. = 0. $\sum$Diff.²
= 178.5

To find Spearman's r, we use the equation:

$$r = 1 - \frac{6\Sigma D^2}{n(n^2 - 1)}$$

In words, this equation directs us to multiply the number of pairs (n) times the square of the number of pairs minus 1, to divide this quantity into the number obtained by multiplying 6 times Σ Difference^2, and to subtract the result from 1. Substituting our heron Σ Difference^2 from Table A2.2 in the equation gives us:

$$r = 1 - \frac{6(178.5)}{15(15^2 - 1)}$$

$$= 1 - \frac{6(178.5)}{15(225 - 1)}$$

$$= 1 - \frac{6(178.5)}{15(224)}$$

$$= 1 - \frac{1071}{2860}$$

$$= 1 - 0.37$$

$$= 0.63$$

So $r = 0.63$. We now wish to test the null hypothesis that there is no relation between catch time and giving-up time, that our calculated r of 0.63 is just due to a chance outcome. As we did in Appendix 1, we will use the 5% level of rejection in comparing our calculated r with that expected solely due to chance. Table A2.3 lists the critical values of r at the 5% level of significance for various numbers of pairs. The r value in Table A2.3 corresponding to a sample size of of 15 pairs is 0.62. Our calculated r of 0.63 is larger, so we reject the null hypothesis. Since the positive correlation between catch time and giving-up time in Great Blue Herons has less than a 5% probability of being due to chance alone, we have proven true our

BEYOND BIRDING

Table A2.3. Values of *r* at the 5% level of confidence. If a calculated *r* is greater than or equal to the corresponding value in the table, we reject the null hypothesis and fail to reject the alternative hypothesis

Number of pairs	Value of *r*
5	1.00
6	0.94
7	0.89
8	0.83
9	0.78
10	0.75
11	0.73
12	0.71
13	0.67
14	0.64
15	0.62
16	0.60
17	0.58
18	0.56
19	0.55
20	0.53
21	0.52
22	0.51
23	0.50
24	0.48
25	0.47
26	0.46
27	0.46
28	0.45
29	0.44
30	0.43

prediction, and we have failed to reject the alternative hypothesis that giving-up time is caused by catch time.

Those knowledgeable in statistics might claim that we could have used a "one-tailed" rather than a "two-tailed" test, since we predicted the direction of the correlation. For the sake of clarity and simplicity, I have chosen to ignore the distinction. In any case, a significant two-tailed correlation will also be significant in a one-tailed analysis.

Doing a little exercise will help you gain isight into the way r is related to the ranking procedure. In our heron example, what values of Difference^2 would give $r = -1, 0$, and $+1$? How would catch times and giving-up times have to be ranked relative to each other to produce these three values of Difference^2?

In summary, to carry out the Spearman Rank Correlation Test:

1. Rank the values of each variable from smallest to largest.
2. Find the difference between ranks for each pairs of numbers Square these differences and sum them to obtain Difference^2.
3. Use the equation to calculate Spearman's r.
4. Compare your calculated r with the r value in Table A2.3 corresponding to your numbers of pairs. If calculated r is equal to or greater than tabulated r, reject the null hypothesis at the 5% level of confidence. If calculated r is less than tabulated r, reject the alternative hypothesis at the 5% level of confidence.

Further reading.

Runyon, R.P. and A. Haber. 1971. Fundamentals of behavioral statistics. Addison-Wesley, Reading, Massachusetts.

Siegel, S. (1956). Nonparametric statistics for the behavioral sciences. McGraw-Hill, New York.

Appendix 3. Scientific Names of the Bird Species Mentioned.

Common Name	Scientific Name
Tropicbird, White-tailed	*Phaethon lepturus*
Gannet, Northern	*Sula bassanus*
Pelican, White	*Pelecanus erythrorhynchos*
Pelican, Brown	*Pelecanus occidentalis*
Heron, Great Blue	*Ardea herodias*
Egret, Great	*Casmerodius albus*
Egret, Cattle	*Bubulcus ibis*
Egret, Snowy	*Egretta thula*
Heron, Little Blue	*Egretta caerulea*
Heron, Green-backed	*Butorides striatus*
Goose, Snow	*Chen caerulescens*
Wigeon, American	*Anas americana*
Vulture, Black	*Coragyps atratus*
Vulture, Turkey	*Cathartes aura*
Osprey	*Pandion haliaetus*
Eagle, Bald	*Haliaeetus leucocephalus*
Hawk, Rough-legged	*Buteo lagopus*
Kestrel, American	*Falco sparverius*
Grouse, Ruffed	*Bonasa umbellus*
Bobwhite, Northern	*Colinus virginianus*
Crane, Whooping	*Grus americana*
Sandpiper, Upland	*Bartramia longicauda*
Sanderling	*Calidris alba*
Sandpiper, Semi-palmated	*Calidris pusilla*

Common Name	Scientific Name
Sandpiper, Least	*Calidris minutilla*
Sandpiper, White-rumped	*Calidris fuscicollis*
Woodcock, American	*Scolopax minor*
Gull, Laughing	*Larus atricilla*
Gull, Herring	*Larus argentatus*
Gull, Ivory	*Pagophila eburnea*
Owl, Snowy	*Nyctea scandiaca*
Kingfisher, Belted	*Ceryle alcyon*
Kingfisher, Green	*Chloroceryle americana*
Woodpecker, Red-headed	*Melanerpes erythrocephalus*
Woodpecker, Acorn	*Melanerpes formicivorous*
Woodpecker, Red-bellied	*Melanerpes carolinus*
Sapsucker, Yellow-bellied	*Sphyrapicus varius*
Woodpecker, Downy	*Picoides pubescens*
Woodpecker, Hairy	*Picoides villosus*
Flicker, Common	*Colaptes auratus*
Woodpecker, Pileated	*Dryocopus pileatus*
Lark, Horned	*Eremophila alpestris*
Swallow, Tree	*Tachycineta bicolor*
Swallow, Bank	*Riparia riparia*
Jay, Blue	*Cyanocitta cristata*
Nutcracker, Clark's	*Nucifraga columbiana*
Crow, American	*Corvus brachyrhynchos*
Chickadee, Black-capped	*Parus atricapillus*
Chickadee, Carolina	*Parus carolinensis*
Chickadee, Boreal	*Parus hudsonicus*
Chickadee, Chestnut-backed	*Parus rufescens*
Titmouse, Tufted	*Parus bicolor*
Tit, Great	*Parus major*
Nuthatch, Red-breasted	*Sitta canadensis*
Nuthatch, White-breasted	*Sitta carolinensis*
Creeper, Brown	*Certhia americana*

Common Name	Scientific Name
Wren, House	*Troglodytes aedon*
Bluebird, Mountain	*Sialia cirrucoides*
Robin, American	*Turdus migratorius*
Starling, European	*Sturnus vulgaris*
Ovenbird	*Seiurus aurocapillus*
Tanager, Scarlet	*Piranga olivacea*
Cardinal, Northern	*Cardinalis cardinalis*
Grosbeak, Rose-breasted	*Pheucticus ludovicianus*
Dickcissel	*Spiza americana*
Towhee, Rufous-sided	*Pipilo erythrophthalmus*
Sparrow, American Tree	*Spizella arborea*
Sparrow, Field	*Spizella pusilla*
Sparrow, Savannah	*Passerculus sandwichensis*
Sparrow, Grasshopper	*Ammodramus savannarum*
Sparrow, Fox	*Passerella iliaca*
Sparrow, Song	*Melospiza melodia*
Sparrow, White-throated	*Zonotrichia albicollis*
Sparrow, White-crowned	*Zonotrichia leucophrys*
Junco, Dark-eyed	*Junco hyemalis*
Bobolink	*Dolichonyx oryzivorus*
Blackbird, Red-winged	*Agelaius phoeniceus*
Meadowlark, Eastern	*Sturnella magna*
Meadowlark, Western	*Sturnella neglecta*
Grackle, Common	*Quiscalus quiscula*
Cowbird, Brown-headed	*Molothrus ater*
Oriole, Northern	*Icterus galbula*
Finch, Purple	*Carpodacus purpureus*
Redpoll, Common	*Carduelis flammea*
Siskin, Pine	*Carduelis pinus*
Goldfinch, American	*Carduelis tristis*
Grosbeak, Evening	*Coccothraustes vespertinus*
Sparrow, House	*Passer domesticus*